LESSONS FROM THE GREATEST STOCK TRADERS OF ALL TIME

JOHN BOIK

McGraw-Hill

New York   Chicago   San Francisco   Lisbon   London
Madrid   Mexico City   Milan   New Delhi
San Juan   Seoul   Singapore
Sydney   Toronto

The *McGraw·Hill* Companies

2 3 4 5 6 7 8 9 0 DOC/DOC 0 1 0 9 8 7 6 5 4

ISBN 0-07-143788-6

McGraw-Hill books are available at special quantity discounts to use as premiums and sales promotions, or for use in corporate training programs. For more information, please write to the Director of Special Sales, McGraw-Hill Professional, Two Penn Plaza, New York, NY 10121-2298. Or contact your local bookstore.

This publication is designed to provide accurate and authoritative information in regard to the subject matter covered. It is sold with the understanding that neither the author nor the publisher is engaged in rendering legal, accounting, or other professional service. If legal advice or other expert assistance is required, the services of a competent professional person should be sought.
—*From a Declaration of Principles jointly adopted by Committee of the American Bar Association and a Committee of Publishers.*

This book is printed on recycled, acid-free paper containing a minimum of 50% recycled, de-inked fiber.

Library of Congress Cataloging-in-Publication Data

Boik, John, 1961-
  Lessons from the greatest stock traders of all time : proven strategies active traders can use today to beat the markets / by John Boik.
     p. cm.
  ISBN 0-07-143788-6 (pbk.)
  1. Stocks. 2. Investments. 3. Stockbrokers. I. Title.

HG4661.B63 2004
332.63'22—dc22

                                            2003024380

CONTENTS

ACKNOWLEDGMENTS

To my wife, Gina, for her understanding and support. To my five-year-old daughter, Daniella. It was a joy to have you by my side, and I thank you for allowing me to share the computer (mine) with you throughout this project.

To a few great friends and my parents for providing continued encouragement.

To the professional staff at McGraw-Hill, especially my fine editor Kelli Christiansen.

Finally, to Mr. William O'Neil. This book would never have been written without the accomplishments he has achieved, especially his dedicated efforts to bring relevant, fact-based, quality market information to the individual investor.

INTRODUCTION

Lessons from the Greatest Stock Traders of All Time is about incredible achievements. It profiles five individuals who attained great levels of success in one of the most difficult endeavors—trading stocks. Although many people make substantial profits and attain some success trading stocks (while most do not), the people described in this book are standout achievers.

They are the greatest because they all achieved (and one is still achieving) enormous success across decades. They paved new ways in stock market success and have stood the test of time. And when the test of time involves the stock market, that makes the achievement that much more impressive.

Who are these people and how did they get to be distinguished as the greatest? They are all Wall Street legends, and each one published at least one book describing his successful trading strategies. Here is a preview.

- Jesse Livermore—The reclusive, private genius whose revolutionary trading strategies are still being used today. Livermore attained incredible wealth and gave it back many times, eventually falling victim to his own personal problems and severe depression.
- Bernard Baruch—The intelligent, sophisticated financier whose trading success earned him great riches and entry into successful financial dealings, and then into public service with the nation's highest levels of power.
- Gerald M. Loeb—The financial writer, stockbroker, and skittish trader who made millions for more than half a century, "battling" the market by staying disciplined to his strict trading rules.
- Nicolas Darvas—The "outsider" whose almost accidental initial first success in stocks led him on a quest of sheer determination

to succeed in stock trading. After many years of trial and error, perseverance never wavering, his efforts finally paid off in millions and landed him a feature story in *Time* magazine.

- William J. O'Neil—The factual, hard-working researcher whose never-ending, detailed study and disciplined trading rules led to fortunes in stock trading. Then, by using his trading profits, he launched successful investment research information businesses serving both professional and individual investors.

Stock trading attracts many people because it's easy to try, and many view it as an easy and quick way to riches. But as the majority learn, most the hard way, it's not as easy at it seems. The stock market is an interesting display of expectations and emotions. It's by looking under the surface and past the daily minor market fluctuations, delving into the details, that these leaders studied and discovered the methods that really worked. This required intense observation and study to succeed at the highest levels, just as any other vocation requires the same attention and hard work to attain great success. This, though, is also where most people fail and do not give adequate attention and effort. As these great traders observed through experience, the stock market is not obvious; it is designed to fool most of the people most of the time.

Every new market cycle always brings out new so-called experts who tout new strategies to try to succeed in the battle of the market. New books are written, new newsletters are printed, and new Web sties tout newfound secrets and supposedly new ways to succeed in the market. However, few survive very long and are gone before we ever get to see a sustained track record of success. And just like any other field such as sports, music, business, medicine, art, etc., there are the few who excel above all others. It's no different when it comes to the stock market. Just like anything worth pursuing in life, it takes hard work and dedication to be able to achieve the highest levels possible.

Lessons from the Greatest Stock Traders of All Time covers these five successful traders, spanning the past century. If we add up all of the years these experts traded in the markets, we cover periods of approximately 1892-1940 (Jesse Livermore), 1897–1930s (Bernard Baruch, when he was most active in the market), 1921–1970s (Gerald M. Loeb), 1952–1960s (Nicolas Darvas), and 1960-present (William J. O'Neil). All told, these time frames cover every year of the market for more than 100 years of organized stock trading through all types of stock market cycles. See, for example, Figure I-1.

Each period offered different market environments, such as strong bull markets and deep bear markets. As a result, there are lessons to learn from these masters that relate to just about every market condition. The strategies they employed were very similar to each other, no matter what time period they traded in. Chapter 6 summarizes the incredible commonalities in their methods, disciplines, and rules. These traders discovered, through their own mistakes and experiences, some common conclusions in the basic strategies and principles that eventually led them to succeed beyond most others in the stock market.

By measuring similarities with the different periods of the market, we prove one very important point concerning the stock market. As the market goes either up or down year after year and business cycle after business cycle, the elements that drive it never really change that much. Why? Because human nature rarely changes. And even though millions of people are involved in the market every day, there are only a handful of human traits that play in the market no matter what day, year, or decade it is. Those human traits include fear, greed, hope, and ignorance. And human nature has a huge impact on the market. After all, the market is consistently comprised of opinions of many different people and market professionals.

A famous observation from Jesse Livermore was, "There is nothing new on Wall Street or in stock speculation. What has happened in the past will happen again and again and again. This is because human

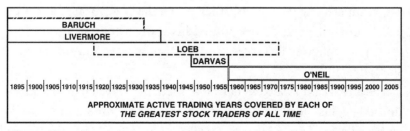

Figure I-1

nature does not change, and it is human emotion that always gets in the way of human intelligence."

So, whether it's 1929 or 1999 or 2029, the market is influenced most by human nature and the human opinions and expectations of future profit potential. It's mastering the human nature element of the market that separates the minority of people who are successful in stock trading from the vast majority of the unsuccessful stock traders.

The names featured in this book are legends on Wall Street. Jesse Livermore and Bernard Baruch were famous during the beginning of the twentieth century. They set new rules and precedents that led them to incredible success and wealth. Though Jesse Livermore experienced many setbacks and hardships along the way, he was truly a market genius and attained both a vast fortune and great personal achievements. He socialized with people at the highest levels of success in the business world. And he has been considered the best trader ever by numerous people over the years.

Bernard Baruch's successes in stock trading led him to great fortune in the business world. He also became a legend as a financier and then enjoyed a successful venture into politics, as he helped draft the treaty of peace and served as the Chairman of the War Industries Board for President Woodrow Wilson during World War I.

Gerald M. Loeb was also a legend on Wall Street, though he traveled a quieter road. He managed to amass millions during a career spanning more than 50 years in the "battlefield" of trading stocks in the marketplace, as well as being a successful stockbroker and financial writer. He also had to compete against the godfather of value investing, Benjamin Graham, as Graham's classic *Security Analysis* hit the bookshelves about the same time in 1935 as Loeb's classic *The Battle for Investment Survival.* The two differing styles of investing competed against each other as Graham advocated the buy and hold strategy and Loeb touted his skittish trading style as the most plausible way to succeed in the stock market and realize substantial profits.

Nicolas Darvas's successful Darvas Method grabbed national attention when his story was featured in *Time* magazine and his self-authored story *How I Made $2,000,000 in the Stock Market* became a national bestseller when it was published in 1960. Darvas's experience proves to all aspiring traders that anyone, even those not directly involved in the securities business, can reap the monetary rewards of the stock market if they put forth the required efforts.

William J. O'Neil is the great modern-day success story. O'Neil built his fortune trading stocks and then funneled his profitable winnings into successful businesses supporting the investment world. His ventures, William O'Neil & Co. serving the institutional investment houses and *Investor's Business Daily* catering to the individual investor, are mainstays. They are respected in today's world as reliable research and investor information sources. O'Neil's "*CAN SLIM*" method has become a favorite of many individual investors.

Numerous publications about these great traders detail their own stories and strategies. Some have become bestsellers, and most reside in serious stock traders' personal libraries, oft regarded as investment classics. This book references many of these published works by and about these great traders. I highly encourage you to read each of their stories for a more detailed look into the lives and trading strategies of these great stock traders. More information about the publications that focus on these five traders can be found in the resources section at the back of this book.

The experiences of the greatest stock traders of all time can teach us many lessons. After all, who better to learn from, in any endeavor, than the ones who attained the highest levels after experiencing all the mistakes, trials, and tribulations, and then formulating winning strategies to overcome them?

So let's begin to profile these great stock traders and find out what separates them from the majority when it comes to the stock market. We will discover how adhering to the strict rules requiring discipline, patience, hard work, and persistence can pay huge rewards. I think you will find these similarities very interesting and, with dedication, by learning from the greats, you too can develop your own rules to go along with the basic time-tested strategies in this book. Perhaps someday in the future you can add your name to the distinguished list of The Greatest Stock Traders of All Time.

1

Jesse Livermore

"It's not the thinking that makes the money; it's the sitting."

The Reclusive Genius

Jesse Livermore was born on July 26, 1877 in Massachusetts. He came from a poor family, as his father struggled as a farmer with the challenging New England soil. Young Jesse knew he wanted more from life, and when his father pulled him out of school to follow in his footsteps, Jesse ran away from home at the age of 14. With just a few dollars in his pocket—given to him by his mother—he headed to Boston. He landed a job as a chalkboard boy for Payne Webber that paid him the minimal wage of $6 per week. His responsibilities in his new job required him to post the stock quotes on big chalkboards covering the length of the brokerage house as prices were called out by tape watchers sitting in the gallery as fast as they could yell them out from the ticker tape machines.

Livermore always excelled at mathematics in school, and he found the tape of the Street to be his calling. He was truly gifted, with a photographic memory when it came to numbers. He actually performed three years of mathematics in one year of school during his youth. He would memorize prices and ticker symbols from his job at Payne Webber. He became a voracious tape reader and watched the tape with total concentration and focus. He also started to keep a notebook of the numbers from his chalkboard job, and he soon noticed that certain patterns emerged. He would keep thousands of price changes in this notebook diary and study them, looking for these certain price patterns. By the time Livermore was 15, he was seriously studying stock patterns and price changes. His "on the job training" allowed him to be ever observant of the activities and how people participated in the market. He noticed that most people lost money in the stock market because they acted randomly, did not act on rules or a predefined plan, and did not put forth the required study that the market and its actions required.

His first trade was made jointly with a friend. They invested a total of $5 in Burlington because Livermore's friend thought the stock would rise. They executed the trade with one of the "bucket shops" in Boston. The atmosphere within the shops was more conducive to low-budget speculation, as one was basically betting on the next move of the stock, or very short term trading. You could also bet on the movement of the stock without actually owning the stock certificates. If the stock moved against you by 10 percent, your trade was wiped out. This was the 10-percent margin rule that was in effect at the time, and it would establish a strict loss-cutting rule for Livermore that he adhered to most of the time during his trading career. Over time and due to experience, he would actually improve on this and he would be able to cut his losses to less than 10 percent.

Concerning Burlington, Livermore first checked his notebook and became convinced that the stock would rise based on its recent trading pattern. So his first stock trade took place when he was 15, and he ended up making a profit of $3.12 on his share of the trade.

He continued to trade in the bucket shops, and by the time he was 16 he was making more money trading than he was making at his job with Payne Webber. When he made a total of $1000 he quit his job to trade full time in the bucket shops.

Livermore made so much money by the time he was 20 that he was banned from the bucket shops of Boston and New York, as he was having an adverse effect on the shop owners' profits. (He would bounce back and forth between the two cities when he would be discovered in one or the other.) His success earned him the nickname "The Boy Plunger." Bucket shop owners wanted nothing to do with him, or his winning trades, which were constantly taking profits from their shops.

With his confidence high he decided to head to New York and trade the stocks on the listed New York Stock Exchange. After all, this was the big time and he was now ready to test his skills in the big league. He set up an account with a brokerage office with $2500 he had as his capital stake. This was down from a high of $10,000 he had attained at one time from his bucket shop trades.

As he lost his profits, Livermore learned the hard way that trading wasn't always easy. As a result, he started to analyze the mistakes he made that caused his losses. This detailed analysis of past mistakes would prove to be a vital trait of his later success. This also became one of his best learning tools.

One of the lessons he discovered during this first analysis period was he would become impatient and thought he had to trade. Impatience in the market usually leads one to making impulse trades, which rarely leads to profitable success. This mistake would cost him dearly, and it is a mistake made by many traders still today.

New York did not produce much success for Livermore. He went broke within six months and had to borrow $500 from his brokerage firm. With money in hand he headed back to the bucket shops to regain his stake. He discovered that the bucket shops would quote prices instantaneously, whereas there was a delay in the New York quotes. His system at the time was based on instant quotes and quick trades. He returned to New York in two days with $2800 and repaid the $500 loan to the brokerage firm.

But upon his return he found it more difficult than he had expected and still found he was only able to break even in New York, so he returned for a final time to the bucket shops. Just when Livermore successfully brought his account up to $10,000 by trading in disguise, the bucket shop owners finally discovered him again and he was banned for good from the shops.

In 1901, now in New York and trading stocks listed on The New York Stock Exchange during a strong bull market, Livermore went long (bought) on Northern Pacific, and he turned his $10,000 into $50,000. Then just as quickly, he gave it all back on two short positions (borrowing stock from your broker in hopes of buying it back at a lower price and profiting from the difference), as he thought the market would break for a short time. Though he lost on these two trades, he was initially right, but the delays due to the huge volume in trying to fill the trades caused his losses when the stocks reversed on him.

It was from this experience that he learned how difficult very short term trading was going to be on The Big Board. Livermore realized he had to learn how to adapt to the different trading environment that separated the instantaneous action of the bucket shops when compared to the more sophisticated processes of organized trading. So once again, by the spring of 1901, Livermore found himself broke. He then discovered a new hybrid bucket shop that had opened for business. He thought he could regain his stake quickly if he traded in these hybrids. For almost a year he successfully regained his capital until he was discovered and banned from these shops as well.

Through it all, the losses Livermore endured taught him that one must experience losing real money in order to learn the correct ways of the market. He stayed persistent in his pursuit of success and kept learning from his mistakes and experience.

It was also at this time that he discovered the time element. The time element in stock trading means that it takes patience, and the road to profitable trading will occur over time, as in trying to master most pursuits. It can also mean understanding how stocks trade. In the bucket shops, the time element was very short and instant, due to the more gambling nature of how the bucket shops were set up and how they operated. In New York the time element meant there was more of a delay as opposed to instant transactions. There was also the fact that once you purchased a stock on The Big Board, you actually took possession of the certificates reflecting the company in which you owned the stock. This time difference between how the bucket shops operated and how The Big Board operated meant one had to react more to future time. This required patience, which would become a strong trait of Livermore's years later and would lead to some of his largest gains. The time element also proved to him that the road to success in stock speculation was indeed going to happen over an extended period of time. It would not happen overnight.

He was certain of this because he had already experienced many ups and downs when it came to his own capital. He achieved some milestones early on. By the age of 15, he made his first $1000. Before turning 21 he made his first $10,000. He got his account up to $50,000, and then gave it all back two days later. He was experiencing the usual ways of the market, but he was determined to stay persistent, as he knew the life of the market was to be his calling.

Livermore made a definition at this point. He defined gambling as anticipating the market, which was very difficult to do, and he saw the odds as being stacked against the individual trader. He defined speculating as having the ability to be patient and react only when market conditions give you the signals to speculate. Here in his early years, he was constantly learning new skills required to achieve great success in the market. He kept refining his rules as he stayed observant and persistent.

Livermore was, at this time, by no means an expert. He kept listening to others and their so-called "tips." He also kept trading too much. Another mistake he was making was taking his profits—especially in a bull market—way too early. At this time he also discovered the importance of the general market and how important it was to learn and understand what the market is doing overall and how it affects most stocks. He had to learn how to interpret what the market was currently doing and at what stage it was currently in, instead of trying to predict what it was going to do in the future.

During these early years Livermore was in a constant learning mode. He discovered that being impatient in the stock market is one of the biggest mistakes one can make. Through experience he would learn to trust the faith in his own judgment. His constant observations would lend credence to his judgment and not allow him to be distracted by the minor fluctuations that would always occur in the market.

Through experience, his strategies began to work and, at age 30, he was becoming more successful in his trading. At this time he developed his probing strategy (discussed in more detail later in this chapter). The other key strategy he implemented was his pyramiding strategy.

Pyramiding was a strategy that would also become a key trading rule of all the other great traders profiled in this book as well. Pyramiding was buying more of a stock as it kept advancing in price. Imagine how different this strategy must have seemed in those early years, as most people are taught to purchase things at lower prices in order to get a bargain, as opposed to paying higher prices. This concept of adding to your most recent purchases when they prove you were right compounds your returns. Livermore discovered that after he would purchase a stock from observing its price action, if the stock kept increasing in price, the action of the stock was proving to him that he had made the right decision. This confirmation of his correct decision was proof enough for him to continue purchasing more of the stock. This compounding effect would only add more to his increasing gains on those particular stocks.

Livermore used probing and pyramiding strategies on the short side of the market in late 1906, as the market was having difficulty keeping a sustained rally in an upward trend. Here he would add more to his short positions as a weak stock kept declining in price. He had so much success being short in the market during the beginning stages of the bear market of 1907, that he had become a millionaire before he turned 31.

Livermore called the crash of 1907 and made $3 million in a single day on October 24th, as he closed out and covered his short positions. In October 1907, J.P. Morgan, then the most influential person on the financial scene, saved Wall Street from near collapse as he injected the market with the required liquidity needed to continue as a viable institution. Morgan even sent a personal message directly to Livermore requesting that he stop shorting the market. The fact that the great J.P. Morgan acknowledged Livermore's action in the market was a true testament to the reputation and impact that Livermore was gaining on the street.

The Great Bear of Wall Street

By this time, Jesse Livermore was indeed establishing himself as a prominent figure on Wall Street. His newfound wealth made Livermore discover that the big money was made in the big swings of the market, earning the nickname "The Great Bear of Wall Street" from his shorting positions that earned him a fortune in the crash of 1907. Throughout these winning years, Livermore reiterated his belief in never-ending stock market analysis and its essential importance to success.

From his successes in the stock market, he began to speculate in the commodities market as well. He became involved with Percy Thomas, who was considered, at that time, the Cotton King. At the time he started socializing with Thomas, Thomas had lost all of his fortune on a few bad trades. But Livermore listened nonetheless, as he knew of Thomas's prior success and that he was still considered the legend of cotton. Thomas convinced Livermore to take a certain position in cotton. As Livermore soon found out, his long position in cotton would cost him nearly his total fortune. He lost many of the millions he had built up on his profitable trades with this transaction on cotton—largely by breaking many of the market rules he spent so much of his early years developing.

Livermore broke his own rules of playing a lone hand and not listening to others. He also broke his loss-cutting rule, as he kept holding on to a losing position. This experience cost him emotionally as well. As he tried to get his money back, he lost even more money in desperate trading. By this point, Livermore was now deeply in debt to many creditors. This only furthered his depression and he began to lose his confidence, which is devastating to a stock trader.

It took many years for Livermore to get back to his winning ways. The markets were mostly flat to down in the years from 1910 through 1914 (the market was actually closed from August 1914 to mid-December 1914 due to the beginning of World War I). Livermore, at this time, was broke, depressed, and owed creditors more than $1 million. The market also offered no great opportunities during these flat years. In order to clear to his head and get back into his game, he decided to declare bankruptcy in 1914. Still down on his luck, in 1915 during a war-time rally in the market, he was given a line of 500 shares with an unlimited price per share from one of the brokerage houses he traded with. For six weeks he did nothing but study the market and watch the tape. He noticed that certain par levels would be established by a stock. This was an old trading principle that he actually used in his bucket shop trading days. A par level would mean that when a stock rose to a round number such as $100 or $200 per share, it more than likely would keep increasing in price as it cleared this par level.

He bought Bethlehem Steel at $98 and watched it passed through $100 and kept rising. He bought another 500 shares as it hit $114 per share. The next day it hit $145 and he sold out for a profit of $50,000 on the 1000 shares. This transaction helped him regain his confidence and got him to stick to his rules again. He brought his account up to $500,000 at one point, and he finished the year of 1915 with $150,000 in his account.

By the end of 1916, Livermore had started shorting the market. The market soon began to decline. Many leading stocks had topped and started to decline in price when the famous "leak" spread that President Wilson was set to offer a peace plan to the Germans. Wall Street would view this as a negative event because it would hurt the wartime economy of supplying goods to foreign nations. Bernard Baruch (featured in Chapter 2), who had become a friend of Livermore's, was also short in the market at this time and was rumored to have made $3 million on the news leak. A Congressional committee was formed to investigate the rumor leak, and Baruch and Livermore were called on to address the committee. Baruch had admitted that he made $470,000 on his short positions during this time, but he vowed it was not due to having advanced information of the rumor. The New York Stock Exchange nonetheless enacted a new rule stating that it was not proper to trade on news leaks. Of course, this ruling was difficult to enforce but it showed the influence of Livermore and Baruch on the market at that time. Livermore himself cleared approximately $3 million in 1916 by being both long during the rising part of the year and short during the later few months, in which the market turned sharply downward.

On April 6, 1917 the United States entered World War I, and after many successes in the market Livermore would begin to pay off all of his previous debts, even though legally through his 1914 bankruptcy filing, he was not obligated to do so. He also, at the age of 40, established a trust account to insure that he would never go broke again.

Regaining Prominence

By 1917 Livermore was now gaining back his once prominent reputation on Wall Street. On May 13, 1917 a *New York Times* article ran called "Exit the Swashbuckling Trader of Wall Street: Present Day Speculator in Stocks Is More of a Student and Economist Than the Sensational Manipulator of Other Years." The article featured both Jesse Livermore and Bernard Baruch and further identified them as major players and influential and successful stock traders on Wall Street.

During the 1920s Livermore determined that experience was one of the key essentials for continued success in the market. His reputation as one of the best and most successful traders on the street was increasing. He was truly living the American dream, becoming a very wealthy man by following his trading rules. He always considered himself a student of the market and thought it was a continuous learning process. Livermore was convinced that no one could ever master the market.

At about this time he began to find out how important it was to discover which stocks were the real leaders of a strong market movement. He would continuously study how leaders would stand out from the crowd and become the real price gainers. His study of the tape and improved understanding of how the market worked led him to refine his industry leader's approach. He would discover that each new major uptrend in the market would produce these new leaders in new leading industries, usually based on the greatest profit expectations. This reiterated to him the importance that fundamentals have in the market and on stock prices. His other discovery of how certain stocks act alike in the same groups and how the leading groups act in conjunction with the general markets would be a key to his even greater success that was coming his way in The Great Crash of 1929.

From the winter of 1928 to the spring of 1929, a full bull market was in session. Livermore was long for the ride up and profited handsomely, and he then began looking for a top in the market. In the early summer of 1929, he sold all his long positions, preferring to sell on the way up. He also thought the market had become overextended. He saw a tremendous rising market, and a market that had begun to change to a sideways trading pattern, rather than the strong rising market it had been. He started to send out his probes on the short side.

Livermore's probing strategy consisted of taking small positions at the beginning of a trade. If a trade turned out to be successful he would add more shares and continue buying (or shorting) as long as the action was proceeding in the way he thought it was to proceed, which was his pyramiding strategy. He always averaged up in price instead of averaging down, which in his day and for most today is the more popular way, but it is not the most profitable way. He would utilize many different brokers so as not to tip his hand to Wall Street, as his trading power and reputation was something that interested many on the street.

As his probing trades started to work, Livermore was certain the market would begin to turn down, as prices had been rising at an incredible rate for quite some time. This is one of the important skills that all the great traders featured in this book employed. When everything seemed fabulous and terrific, they would always look for signs in the market that things were about to change.

The market in 1929 gave plenty of signals of crashing beforehand. The leaders of the day stopped making new price highs and started to stall. The smart money at that time was beginning to sell into the strength. Also, just about everyone was on 10-percent margin and everybody started giving stocks tips and thought they had became stock market experts. This overexuberance is a clear signal that when everyone is invested in the market, there is simply no more buying power left to continue moving the market higher.

When the market finally crashed in October 1929, Livermore held many shares in short positions he had been building over the previous months. He netted a multimillion-dollar profit on The Great Crash of 1929 when he covered his short positions. When just about everyone else was wiped out due to margin calls and others were rumored to be jumping out of office buildings, Livermore had one of his greatest paydays ever. He was actually blamed for the crash by many, from his prior reputation as "The Great Bear of Wall Street," and he received many death threats from people who had lost everything they had. The New York Times even ran an article with the headline "Jesse Livermore Reported to Be Heading Group Hammering High-Priced Securities..." shortly after the Crash began.

Following the crash, Congress passed the Securities and Exchange Act, forming the Securities Exchange Commission in hopes of providing stability and order to the markets by making sweeping changes regarding stock trading. Despite those changes, Livermore came to the conclusion that he would not have to change his own rules because human nature would not change and it was human nature that ultimately controlled what happened in the stock market.

Though Livermore made many millions on the short side of the market, as he did in 1929, it is usually more difficult to achieve superior results shorting stocks due to the unlimited potential loss one could experience. A rising stock can keep going higher, but a declining stock can only go to zero. It also takes stronger control of your emotions to successfully trade short. You also must be able to react quicker, as fear is the driving force behind price declines and hope is the driving force behind price increases. Because fear instills a quicker reaction than hope, you must be able to react to swifter changes in the overall psychology of the market.

Jesse Livermore, even though he achieved great wealth, still faced many personal challenges throughout his life. Through difficult marriages, divorces, and other family problems, Livermore became severely depressed. He did not achieve as much success in his trading during the 1930s as he did in previous periods, growing more and more depressed about his personal problems. In fact, in 1934 he filed bankruptcy one more time, as it was rumored that he had lost the fortune he had made just five years earlier. This depression, caused by the personal problems in his life, proves how important it is to have one's emotional mind-set in balance to consistently perform for profits in the market and avoid costly mistakes. Many of these later times in his life were in stark contrast to how he disciplined his lifestyle when he was at the top of his game earning his successful reputation on Wall Street.

A Chronicle of Success

In late 1939, he decided to write his own book about his trading strategies, and in March 1940 Livermore's book entitled *How to Trade in Stocks* was published. The book did not sell well, mostly because there was little interest in the stock market at that time due to the lingering effects of the Great Depression. The original work is, however, a great resource for all aspiring traders to study.

Just months after the publication of his book, on November 28, 1940 Jesse Livermore, in a deep depression, committed suicide. He died instantly from a self-inflicted gunshot wound.

For Livermore, the stock market was the greatest, most complex challenge in the world. His desire and passion was in beating the game of Wall Street. Livermore believed that stock speculation was more an art form than pure scientific reason.

Jesse Livermore is regarded by many as probably the greatest stock trader ever. The investment classic *Reminiscences of a Stock Operator*, originally published in 1923 by Edwin Lefevre, is the fictionalized biography of Jesse Livermore's life. *Reminiscences* remains one of the most widely read and highly recommended investment books to this day. Richard Wyckoff wrote a short book entitled *Jesse Livermore's Methods of Trading in Stocks* derived from an interview he did with Livermore in the 1920s. The work details many of Livermore's unique trading strategies. Many other articles and books have been written about Jesse Livermore over the years, as his legendary life continues to generate interest today.

Livermore was a unique individual who paved the road for many traders with his discoveries of what worked and what did not work in the stock market. He was a reclusive and private man, always keeping secret his trades and records. He was one of the first to buy stocks making new highs and breaking through resistance points. This strategy was contrary to others who believed it was best to buy stocks as low and as cheap as possible. Livermore always said he lost money when he broke his own rules and he always made money when he followed them. He worked incredibly hard at analyzing the market and studying speculative theories, and he disciplined his lifestyle to be at peak performance at all times. He made all the mistakes that most make in the market, but he learned from them and he constantly kept learning even more by reading the tape and studying the market.

His famous saying that has been quoted by many sources over the years is that "Wall Street never changes. The pockets change, the stocks change, but Wall Street never changes because human nature never changes." This statement describes the importance psychology plays in the market. He believed that people have acted and reacted the same way in the market due to hope, fear, greed, and ignorance, which is why the numerical formations and patterns of stocks recur on a consistent basis over time.

Livermore also believed that the market was one of the hardest things to be successful at because it involved many people and human nature. It involved anticipating trends and future direction. It was most difficult because controlling and conquering human nature is a very difficult task. Livermore was so interested in the psychological aspect of the market that at one point he the even took psychology courses, just as he had studied securities. Taking these courses proved how dedicated Livermore was to understanding every aspect of the market, even those areas that might not have seemed related to the securities business by most. Livermore would look for every advantage he could in trying to enhance his skill set.

Livermore was actively involved in stock trading for a total of 48 years from 1892 to 1940. Through his many years of experience that included numerous ups and downs, bankruptcy, and incredible wealth, he developed several strategies to gain success in the market.

The Livermore Way: Setting Standards in Trading Rules

Jesse Livermore's strategy evolved over the many years he traded stocks. In fact, trading stocks was his only real career. Through both many setbacks and positive experiences, he perfected and constantly kept learning what worked and what did not work in the stock market.

Below, we'll discuss the strategies he devised, which many of the great traders following him also implemented in their own trading rules.

Skills and Traits of the Successful Trader

Livermore believed there were certain traits that were required of the successful trader, and that trading was definitely not suited for every-one. It was a vocation not for the stupid, the mentally lazy, or those of inferior emotional balance and especially not for those who expect to get rich quickly. This was an important point for Livermore.

One of the keys to successful trading was in understanding the time element mentioned earlier. Livermore respected the time element insofar that he believed that no one should use the market as a get-rich-quick mechanism. Viewing the market that way was extremely dangerous and usually produced the exact opposite results. Emotional balance, something Livermore later in his life struggled with and that ultimately led to his tragic death, was vitally important, as success in the stock market was more of an emotional battle than an intellectual battle.

One of the qualities that Livermore believed is required for successful trading is poise. He knew that a healthy state of mental balance—one that was not to be influenced by hopes or fears—is a key skill of the successful trader. Patience, which means waiting for the right opportunity, is another required skill. The lack of patience in a trader is a weakness and a major cause of losses. Also, being silent and keeping to yourself about your losses and your gains is a crucial skill. The work ethic to constantly study the market is also essential.

Livermore viewed stock speculation as a full-time job because it requires someone's full attention in order to excel. Just as successful doctors or lawyers need to be trained well and study hard in their professions, stock traders are no different. Most people don't view the stock market as something that requires as much effort as the other professions mentioned. Most view the market as easy and effortless because in order to participate, all one needs to do is to instruct a broker to enter a trade. Or one just needs to hear a tip from an outsider and then act on that information by placing a trade and waiting for the money to arrive. Whereas no one in his right mind would allow you to perform surgery on him or defend him in court without the proper training and certifications, the same should hold true in stock trading. It is definitely a skill that must be perfected over time. Livermore treated stock trading as a business and constantly looked for new ways to improve his skill set.

Areas of expertise he thought essential were:

- Emotional control (controlling the psychological aspects that affect every trader).

- Knowledge of economics and fundamentals of business conditions (the wisdom necessary to understand how certain events can have an impact on the market and stock prices).

- Patience (the ability to let your profits run is what separates the great traders from the mediocre traders).

Four other key skills and traits he thought were required were:
- Observation—stay focused only on factual data.

- Memory—remember key events so you don't repeat prior mistakes.

- Mathematics—understand the numbers and fundamentals. This was a gift and strength of Livermore.

- Experience—learn from your experiences and errors.

The Disciplined Trader

The honesty and sincerity of accurate record keeping, doing your own thinking, and reaching and making your own decisions were all vital disciplines according to Livermore. Every time he did not make his own decisions, he lost money.

Livermore did an extensive review of all his trades, especially the losses. This was one of his most determined traits and one he started early in his career. This review of past trades was the best learning mechanism for him in order to avoid future losses and repeating prior mistakes.

Another discipline Livermore started later (and if he had done so sooner likely would have helped him avoid some of his lowest moments) would be to take half of his profits, usually on trades where he doubled his money, and put them in a cash reserve. This reserve would serve him well in avoiding bankruptcy. It also supplied needed capital when the market would turn, and he could use it to take advantage of changing market situations.

Another key lesson Livermore learned early on was that trading every day and or every week is a loser's game and cannot be done with much success. He learned there were many times to make money trading stocks and there were times when you should not trade at all. It was healthy for him to take many breaks and vacations when the market did not offer its best opportunities. This discipline forced him to not trade all the time. By staying on the sidelines and being observant, one can see more clearly the major changes than if one were constantly observing minor fluctuations day in and day out.

Livermore was always very vigilant about his constant quest for reading the tape and analyzing the price movements of the market and individual stocks. The discipline he applied to his trading and how seriously he applied himself is legendary. He studied in private during the early morning hours at his residence, usually putting in an hour or two before breakfast. This quiet time alone with no interruptions was very important to him. After being well rested from the night before, he found this early morning ritual a great mental exercise for himself. He could analyze economic conditions, the news of the prior day, and then determine the appropriate actions he believed he would take and how the market might react.

His reclusive nature would allow no outside influences from others contradicting his thought process. At his office he would allow no talking from his help during the day, and he made sure he would stand for most of the day. He would do this to get a clear view of the tape and also because he believed a perfect posture from standing upright allowed him to think more alertly. His desk was said to be always immaculate as far as papers and how it was organized. Livermore clearly disciplined his trading life to be at peak performance.

Pioneering New Trading Rules

Livermore was a pioneer in many of the trading rules he implemented. He really did not have anyone else before him who experienced great success in order for him to learn from. Livermore learned from his mistakes, and he studied the market with total concentration and utilized his experience to discover what worked and what did not when it came to the stock market. Trial and error and experience paved the way for many other traders in the following years to learn from his strategies.

Many traders came to follow the basic principles Livermore employed, often learning the rules through their own mistakes. For instance, Livermore was presumed to be one of the first traders to buy stocks when they hit new highs in price. He would make purchases when a stock made a new high on increased volume after experiencing a normal correction or reaction. The same rules would apply to shorting stocks, as he would take his short positions as weak stocks kept hitting new lows. He would never buy a stock making new lows, and he learned over time to never average down in price by buying more of stock as it began to decline in price. This strategy, called dollar cost averaging, is a losing strategy and one that none of the great traders featured in this book followed.

Livermore was not a chartist, because he read the tape and price movements. Even without using charts, a skilled tape reader still knows when active stocks are about to or were hitting new higher prices. Livermore was a skilled tape reader, which is a very difficult art to master. Tape reading is very difficult because of the constant viewing that is required, and it can become very emotional. It takes extreme discipline and strong rules to avoid getting "caught up" in the tape. The greatest tape readers (Livermore, Jack Dreyfus, and Gerald Loeb) all would rely on the feel they received from the tape through their experience, as opposed to getting caught up in the emotional trap of the tape.

Livermore also applied mathematical analysis as his tool for evaluation, but he mostly received all the information he needed by concentrating on the price and volume action of the tape. A strong confirmation to him, in the possible purchase of a stock, was when a stock was making an all-time high with a noticeable increase in volume accompanying the increase in price. This is a strong indication that the demand for the stock is solid. Volume was a clear indicator to Livermore. He thought that high volume in either individual stocks or in the general market indicated that a change in direction was most likely confirmed. He would attempt to take full advantage of these volume clues as they were presented to him. Volume would be a clear signal for Livermore to implement quality buy-and-sell rules.

He viewed these volume increases as alerts that something was happening. It probably didn't matter to him what it was, as the action of the tape was sufficient enough evidence. He thought that if the trend was that strong, then that was all the proof he needed. He didn't really need to try to discover the exact reason why many investors had finally decided to have a strong demand for a particular stock. If the move was to the upside, the trend would likely take the stock higher. If the move was to the downside, it would likely take it lower. That confirmation would be a signal to him that it was time for him to act. His trading decisions were based on the probability of the next move and a current change in the trend.

These purchases made at new highs could not be made without other vital factors in place. Livermore realized that you had to make the purchase at just the right time. For example, he would look for prices breaking through resistance levels. This price action occurs when a stock breaks through an area where it had previously been trading and creates a new line of least resistance. He would determine the line of resistance at the moment of trading and then wait for the moment when that line defines itself. This was viewed as the perfect psychological time to enter a trade at the beginning of a major market move or a change in the basic trend. This could occur either in an individual stock or the general market. It also didn't matter to him in which direction this action would occur, as he played both sides of the market.

He would then observe the action of the stock closely to see if the trend in the movement continued in that direction. If it did, then the movement was confirmed with this continuation and the new trend was underway. It is not wise to chase a stock too far past this point, as the risks are usually too great at that time for failure. (This is similar to how O'Neil views chasing after extended stocks discussed in Chapter 5.) It is also not prudent to buy before this move occurs, as this might prove to be premature because the stock, might never move in the desired direction. Livermore wanted the action of the stock going through these key points to lead him into new positions. He used these rules for short positions as well. If a stock traded at a new low and it formed at a certain point (rallied from a new low and then dropped through to a new low), he would think that most likely the fall would continue and he would establish a short position in the stock.

Buying at new highs after stocks had made minor reactions or corrections and then breaking through these areas was an action he called "breaking through the line of least resistance." It correlates to a body in motion. Once a stock breaks through its line of least resistance, it is free to continue in the new direction or trend. Livermore thought the stock at this point had the greatest chance to proceed upward in price, if he was long on the stock. Again, it is important to wait for these actions to occur before making a trade. This would confirm for him that the market was going to move in a certain direction. This strategy would act as a risk-controlled mechanism for him.

This action was also the beginning of the psychological move of a market trend. If the market would not continue in that direction, he knew it was a wrong move and he would cut his losses short and exit the trade. Waiting for that action was very important. This required a great deal of patience. He would sit on cash for as long as it took before he would commit money.

Volume action also must be studied closely as it continues, so as to observe when the trend stops moving in the proper direction. Because the market always moves reflecting many investor decisions, this does not mean that minor and normal corrections and reactions don't occur.

Another important key in Livermore's trading rules was to concentrate only on the leaders of a new bull market. He also kept the number of stocks he followed small and manageable. And he waited for the market to confirm the leadership before committing to the trade. He concentrated on the leading groups instead of spreading himself all over the market. He noticed that the leading stocks of the new leading groups were usually the strongest stocks. He avoided the weak industries and the weak stocks within those industries. This proved his avoidance of cheap stocks. He observed that weak, declining stocks recover with great difficulty and he confined his activity to the active stocks that were moving.

He would stay observant of the market and linked stock price movements of a leading stock to others within its industry. Also, in the leading groups he noticed that if a particular stock did exceptionally well, some of its peers in the same group would also do well. Noticing this was an important factor in the movement of prices, he would often watch many stocks within the same group to monitor their actions. He believed that prospects would work alike with most stocks of a given group. He would call this the manifest group-tendency. If during a strong market a certain group was experiencing stocks not acting in a strong way, he would usually sell out any positions he had in that group or avoid stocks within that group altogether.

Livermore would always watch other stocks in the same industry in which he made his trades to observe unforeseen circumstances. He would notice that if one particular leader in a strong group started to act adversely, the other stocks in the group would normally start to act the same way. This constant observation always kept him apprised as to what was happening within the leading industry groups and the general market.

He would also notice how certain groups would have seasonal patterns to them. It is important to understand how economic cycles play into certain industries and how their cycles can affect stock prices. One must also understand that the stock market usually discounts seasonal activities in advance. Therefore, it is crucial to be able to foresee certain industry conditions many months in advance. This understanding reinforces the need to constantly be observant and to be aware of economic and fundamental conditions.

One of the ways in which Livermore called the tops of the 1907 and the 1929 markets was because the leading stocks and the leading groups weakened months before the actual market indexes crashed. He deduced that when the leaders begin to roll over, one should look out, as the rest of the market usually follows. In 1929, the lessons he learned from the 1907 crash allowed him to take full advantage of the market clues, and through his experience, he realized some of his largest profits.

Livermore also discovered that when the leaders usually top and roll over, he would not try to always understand why. He let the market make the moves. He wouldn't waste time trying to figure out why a stock declined, all he had to know was just that it did decline and that he needed to act accordingly. The why, he discovered, will usually come out later, as the stock market almost always discounts future news.

To correctly buy the leading stocks in the leading industry groups after they break through their lines of least resistance, and make sure he was on the correct side of the market, Livermore implemented his probing and pyramiding strategies.

Before implementing a trade however, it is wise to understand the trend of the general market. Livermore believed that the market would blend the future into the present, and that is why it was always difficult to accurately predict what the market will do in the future. The market would always do what it wanted to do and not what it was expected to do. He would be long in a bull market, short in a bear market, and during sideways markets he would stay in cash until a confirmed trend one way or another was established. Discovering this change in trend was one of the hardest things to do because it went against what was currently being thought and acted on at the time. This is why he started using his probe strategy.

Livermore's probing and pyramiding strategies worked by taking partial positions in a stock until he reached the total number of shares he initially intended to purchase. It was very important for Livermore to decide how much of a stock he was going to buy before he actually started buying. This is a product of good money management planning, which was one of Livermore's key rules. He would take a small position at first to test the stock, which was the probing strategy, and then see if his initial research was correct. If the stock worked out in the way he had planned, he would buy more, but he would always make sure each successive buy would occur at a higher price.

For example, if he knew he was going to purchase 400 or 500 shares of a certain stock, he would first wait for all the other conditions of his rules to be in place. Then he would purchase one-fifth of his intended purchase or 100 shares (in this example), or only 20 percent of his initial position in the stock. If the stock moved against him he would sell it and take a small loss. If it drifted for a few days, he would also exit, as it did not perform as he thought it would. If the stock moved up in price he would make another purchase. This second purchase would be at a higher price than the first purchase and would be for another 100 shares, or another 20 percent of his original planned position.

At this point he would now own 200 shares of a rising stock that was acting in the way he had thought it should act. This is very important. This removes many of the emotions from the process. His rules would guide him, based on how the stock was acting in the market. He did not rely on hope, fear, or greed. His rules would dictate if he would continue to purchase more shares or begin to exit the stock because it would start to decline.

If the stock, in this example, kept moving up in price, he would buy the remaining shares, or in this case the balance of either 200 or 300 shares. This is how he would manage his risk in a particular issue. It was by constant observation of the price action and following the trend of that action.

This strategy requires very detailed observation, but again it's not supposed to be easy. Livermore's dedication to tape reading and experience produced incredible results as he refined these strategies and adhered to them on his way to producing profitable results.

Once Livermore established his positions, either on the long side or the short side, he would then begin to look for sell signals. It is often said that the hardest part of stock trading is not the buying—it's the selling. It was no different in Livermore's day.

Livermore liked to sell as a stock kept advancing in price. Again, this is extremely hard to do, as it goes against the emotion of greed that would probably be dominating your thoughts as your winning position kept providing you more profits. It's the disciplined traders through experience and knowledge who know through constant market observation how to remove the emotion and take advantage of the right time to exit the position. He knew he could not sell at the absolute top, so he again kept his vision on the tape and looked for signals to sell after a stock had risen for quite some time and then displayed abnormal price and volume action. Little upward price movements on increases in volume and large price declines on increased volume are some key selling signals today that also applied in Livermore's day. Experience plays a large role in knowing how to distinguish abnormal price and volume behavior.

Livermore would normally only enter a long position if he saw at least a probable profit of 10 points or more. Many of his big winners were much larger than that, as his patience in sticking with them paid off. However, many of his trades did not go the way he initially intended them to go. If the stock began to move down, he would sell

out at a minimal loss of a few points. This action was a confirmation
to him that his judgment was probably wrong. In the stock market,
when you are wrong the best way to correct it is to do something
about it. In Livermore's case, it was to sell and move on to something
else. If the stock drifted and didn't move much, he would also close
out his position, as this represented an opportunity cost to him. He
would rather be in stocks that are active and moving in one direction
or another.

Most of Livermore's strategies and rules were based on thinking
differently about the market than most others did in his day. His main
strategies could be summarized by the following:

- Understand the general trend of the market. You must be in tune
  with what the market is currently doing and be observant of it at
  all times. Watch and move with the market; don't fight against it.

- Buy stocks hitting new highs in price as they pass through certain resistance areas. Use a probing strategy to test your moves
  and pyramid additional buys on increases in price.

- Cut your losses short. Protect yourself from a wrong decision at
  no more than a 10-percent loss. Sell drifting stocks, as their inac-
  tion is an opportunity cost.

- Let your profits ride, as your strongest stocks keep moving up or
  down (if in short positions). Be patient with stocks that are acting correctly. The big money is made by sitting tight.

- Leading stocks in leading and strong industries is where your
  concentration should be.

- Avoid tips and information from others. Conduct your own
  homework, stick with the facts, and understand the fundamentals.

- Avoid cheap stocks. The big money is made in the big swings,
  and they usually don't come from cheap stocks.

Especially in Livermore's day, these rules were viewed as totally
inaccurate and wrong. However, the success and wealth that Jesse Livermore attained proved in the end that these were the right strategies
to implement.

Proven Strategies Applied Today

To prove how the market doesn't really change over time and how stocks repeat similar patterns, the following charts illustrate how Livermore's strategies could be applied to the current market environment. Beginning in mid-March 2003, the market started a convincing uptrend following the brutal bear market that began in March 2000. After three years of declining prices, the market confirmed its new uptrend with new leaders taking charge. Improved economic conditions and forecast improvements in corporate profitability set the stage for a classic uptrend that, as of this writing, has passed its six-month anniversary.

Several professional money managers today do utilize strategies that Jesse Livermore pioneered back in his day. One of the new emerging leaders of the March 2003 uptrend was Stratasys, Inc. (SSYS). Stratasys is a technology company that develops, manufactures, and markets 3-D rapid prototyping devices that create physical models from computerized designs. Stratasys also is a leading, fundamentally strong stock, as its quarter ended December 2002 showed an 81-percent increase in earnings and a 13-percent increase in revenues. The quarter ended March 2003 showed even better performance—a 243-percent increase in earnings and a 67-percent increase in revenues.

Figure 1-1 illustrates the action of the stock from January 2003 through March 2003 and notes key areas where Livermore's strategies could have alerted the observant trader. Even though Livermore was a tape reader as opposed to a chartist, the chart illustrates clearly how his strategies could have been used to identify a strong new market leader as the general trend of the market turned up and began a strong rally.

In Figure 1-1 we see the following points when implementing strategies from Livermore:

- Waiting for the general market to turn upward (market confirmed uptrend on March 17, 2003).
- Looking for new leaders breaking through resistance points (Stratasys broke through $13 for the first time in over three years).
- Volume playing a major role in the stock breaking through the resistance point, confirming the demand for the stock.

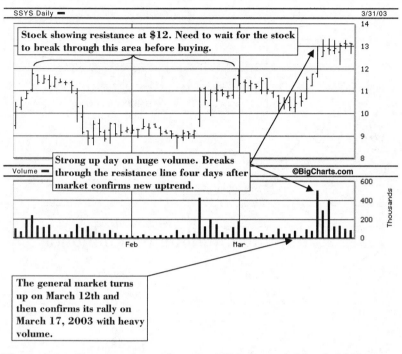

Figure 1-1   Stratasys, Inc.—January 2003 through March 2003.

Source: *www.bigcharts.com.*

Figure 1-2 illustrates more key trading rules of Livermore as we watch the progression of Stratasys for the next three month period—April 2003 through June 2003.

Figure 1-2 shows how using additional strategies from Livermore with this new leading stock could lead to profitable gains such as:

- Being patient with a confirmed leading stock and letting it con-solidate its gains.

- Utilizing the pyramiding strategy to add to winning positions if the stock is acting as you expected.

- Holding tight and not being tempted into taking short-term profits as long as the stock and the general market are acting as you expected.

Purchasing Stratasys on March 21, 2003 at the closing price of $13 would have yielded a 166-percent profit by June 30, 2003 as Stratasys

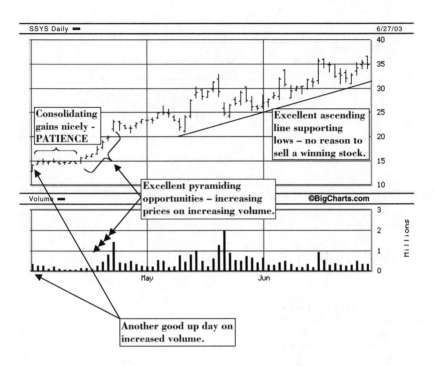

Figure 1-2   Stratasys—April 2003 through June 2003.

Source: *www.bigcharts.com.*

closed that day at $34.58. It's important to note that waiting for the general market to confirm its uptrend is crucial. The NASDAQ (the leading index of the uptrend) staged a reversal pivotal point on March 12th when it closed up 7.7 points to finish at 1279.23 on an increase in volume. The confirming strength came the very next day when the NASDAQ shot up 61.54 points to close at 1340.73 on an even larger increase in volume. The next day showed a small pullback of only .45 points in the index. This is constructive action considering the prior day showed such a large increase. The following session (Monday, March 17th) was the convincing confirmation (see Chapter 5— William J. O'Neil and his assessment of market confirming action) when the NASDAQ zoomed up 51.95 points on even greater volume.

The NASDAQ average was up 27.6 percent from its low of 1271.46 on March 11th to its close of 1622.80 on June 30, 2003. As the market continued its uptrend, Stratasys and the NASDAQ continued gaining ground. On September 30, 2003 the NASDAQ stood at 1786.93, up

40.5 percent from the low it established on March 11th. Stratasys closed at $42.62 on September 30th or 227.9 percent from its breakthrough point on March 17, 2003.

Looking at the same time period we just analyzed, we can view another strong leader of the most recent uptrend. *Netease.com* (NTES) is a China-based Internet company that develops applications, services, and technologies for the Chinese Internet market. China has been viewed as a fast-growing economy and many Chinese consumers have adopted the Internet. The ADR (American Depository Receipts) shares of *Netease.com* trade on the NASDAQ market, and the Internet group that *Netease.com* is a part of was one of the leading industry groups of this uptrend. Figures 1-3 and Figure 1-4 take us through a similar analysis as we saw with Stratasys.

With *Netease.com* we see similar patterns we saw with Stratasys. We see a new leader breaking through a resistance area on large volume shortly after the general market starts an impressive uptrend.

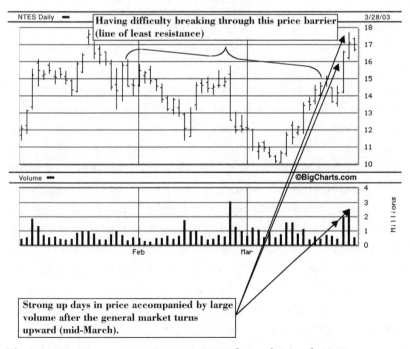

Figure 1-3   *Netease.com.* January 2003 through March 2003.

Source: *www.bigcharts.com.*

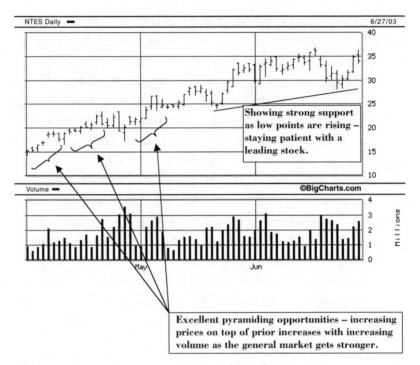

Figure 1-4   *Netease.com.* April 2003 through June 2003.

Source: *www.bigcharts.com.*

Netease.com also exhibits very strong fundamentals. The quarter ended December 31, 2002 showed a 207-percent increase in earnings and an 815-percent increase in revenues. The quarter ending March 31, 2003 produced a 486-percent increase in earnings and a 392-percent increase in revenues. Clearly, this is a dynamic company in a growing market segment that has attracted the attention of large institutional traders that are accumulating positions in a new leader during a new market uptrend. *Netease.com,* if purchased at $16.60 on March 26, 2003, was up 119.7 percent as of June 30, 2003, when it closed at $36.47. By September 30, 2003 *Netease.com* was $55.86 per share, or up 236.5 percent from the breakthrough point in March.

As you read about the other great traders that follow, you'll discover that the strategies and rules Livermore implemented were repeated by most of the others and were key strategies to their success in the stock market.

2

Bernard Baruch

"...even being right three or four times out of ten should yield a person a fortune if he has the sense to cut his losses quickly on the ventures where he has been wrong."

Dr. Facts

Bernard Baruch was born in 1870 in South Carolina. He graduated from the College of the City of New York and he began his Wall Street career in 1891 when he joined A.A. Housman & Company, a small brokerage firm in New York, as an office boy, runner, and general utility man that paid him $5 per week.

In order to try to advance in his career and move up in the firm, he decided to take night classes in bookkeeping. Through his studies he learned how to analyze the financial aspects of a company. He also started reading *The Financial Chronicle* on a regular basis. He read constantly about many subjects, always trying to learn more, especially concerning the subject of finance. He also began to speculate in stocks on his own. Back then the margin rate was only 10 percent (same as listed in Chapter 1 for Livermore), allowing for an individual to put up only 10 cents on the dollar when purchasing stocks.

Baruch's original trading started out like most, consisting of a few wins and then giving it all back due to a lack of knowledge, experience, sound rules, and discipline. Baruch struggled with his trading in these early years and didn't make much progress. His trades were made mostly by buying small stakes on margin, usually 10 shares each, on the Consolidated Stock Exchange. Most of his trades were in industrial and railroad stocks. He even, like Livermore, tried his hand at the bucket shops in New York. However, Baruch found he was not very successful when it came to the quick action of the bucket shops.

His first major mistake in the speculation business was taking a tip from an outsider about a railroad venture. This venture was to build a tramway to a Put-in-Bay (an island in Lake Erie) hotel. He was so excited about it that he also convinced his father to invest $8000 in the venture. Baruch ended up losing every dollar as the venture failed. Even though his father showed confidence in him and offered him another loan shortly thereafter for $500, Baruch took the experience of this first major loss very personally. As with most traders, Baruch found out you had to lose money in order to try to better yourself.

This loss taught him a valuable lesson. He started analyzing his losses to try to determine the mistakes that were made in causing these losses. This was for him, as it was for Jesse Livermore, a discipline he continued throughout his trading career. This self-analysis became a great learning tool for him as well. For Baruch, the evidence of his losses became clear to him. He thought that most of his losses stemmed from a lack of knowledge of what he was investing in, such as the company's fundamentals and what the company's prospects were for future growth and profits.

The other factor he attributed to his losses was that he was trading beyond his financial resources. He found out it was impossible to run up a fortune on a shoestring and that real success in the stock market was going to take time. How true success in the market occurs over a longer time frame, as opposed to quick riches, became evident to him just as it had to Livermore.

As Baruch continued his trading and learning, he began to discover how the market actually worked. For example, a panic in 1893 caused a depression that affected the railroads and lasted until 1895. During these early years, in 1893, Baruch became a bond salesman with his firm. This depression era caused him to be more cautious toward his clients' trading accounts than he was in his own trading.

One discovery he did make during this time was how large financial gains can be made when the economy emerges from a depression period. During periods of the 1890s and early 1900s, depressionlike and recessionary economic times were commonplace. And recessionary periods would last much longer than they have in more modern times. After experiencing a few of these economic cycles, Baruch would see value in purchasing stocks when panics hit and when stocks were at low depression prices. He always knew, from his careful observation experiences, that a recovery would come along and good opportunities were there for the ever-observant speculator. But as many discover, Baruch found out that the education process takes time.

In 1895 his salary was increased from $5 per week to $25 per week, but after four years on Wall Street he still had little to show in terms of accumulated personal financial assets. His raise in salary actually induced him to more unprofitable trading. He was still overtrading and this caused him to go broke many times. Each market fluctuation would cause him to trade more, which led to still more losses. This was one of the early pitfalls that Jesse Livermore also experienced. The results Baruch was achieving were discouraging to him, but he pressed on and vowed to keep learning. After begging for an even larger increase in his salary, Baruch was given an eighth of an interest in the firm. This made him a partner in the firm, at the young age of 25. He was quickly starting to climb in rank, his job performance viewed positively by top management. These early years would also prove to be his training ground in trading. He even lost every cent of a $6000 bonus he earned at Housman during his first year as partner.

At Housman, Baruch would also work deals in trying to buy control of other firms for his clients' companies. His firm would receive commissions on the transactions for purchasing large amounts of stock in trying to gain control of the companies he was targeting. After a few successful deals, his share in the firm was increased to a one-third ownership position.

In 1897, Baruch purchased 100 shares on margin of American Sugar Refining after researching the company before making his purchase. As the stock rose throughout the next six months, he used his earnings on the stock to buy more. This pyramiding on the way up in price is what also became a profitable trading tool for Livermore, as we saw in Chapter 1. Baruch kept buying as the stock kept rising in price, and he watched his position closely, careful not to let the gain turn on him. When Baruch finally sold out, he had made a profit of $60,000. At that point he bought a seat on the New York Stock Exchange for $19,000 but ended up giving the seat to a relative in need, due to financial difficulties, before he had taken title to it. This success on American Sugar Refining was the turning point for Baruch in becoming a successful speculator.

Due to the success of his firm in 1899, he made enough money to buy another seat on the New York Stock Exchange. He purchased this one for $39,000. This transaction caused his confidence to increase, as his name would now be listed among the elite members of the stock exchange. The earnings for A.A. Housman that year amounted to $501,000. Baruch's share, because he was a one-third partner, came to $167,000. It seemed he was well on his way to a very successful and financially rewarding career. But soon thereafter he purchased American Spirits Manufacturing Company at $10 per share on a tip and put most of his money on it. It declined to the point of nearly wiping him out in just a few short weeks, as the price dropped from 10.25 on June 13, 1899 to 6.25 on June 29 a few weeks later. This was a devastating blow to his just recent success and caused a temporary loss in his confidence. The lesson he learned here was not to buy from tips or others' recommendations and to always establish a cash reserve for future opportunities. He indeed concluded that the main difference in his prior success with American Sugar Refining and this current loss with American Spirits Manufacturing was directly related to one (the gain) benefiting from his own research and the other (the loss) being caused by a lack of effort and fact-based research on his behalf.

As he kept learning and his trading became more successful, Baruch termed trading in stocks as speculation, which comes from the Latin word *speculari*, which means to spy on and observe. He defined a speculator as a man who observes the future and acts before it occurs. Acting swiftly in the market is a key to success. One must search through a maze of complex and contradictory details to get to the significant facts. Then he must be able to operate coldly, clearly, and skillfully on the basis of those facts that are presented before him. The challenge for the successful speculator, he stated, is how to disentangle the cold hard facts from the rather warm feelings of the people dealing with the facts.

Baruch often said his career on Wall Street was one long process of education in human nature. He viewed the market as a makeup of people trying to read the future, which can become very emotional. This discipline of dealing with the facts earned him the nickname "Dr. Facts" from his relationship later on with President Theodore Roosevelt.

Research is a Virtue

After his $60,000 loss in American Spirits, Baruch made a quick comeback with a $60,000 profit in Brooklyn Rapid Transit Co. (B.R.T.) after he righted his tips error. This time he did his own research, and with this comeback he began to regain his confidence.

As his trading continued, Baruch shorted Amalgamated Copper in 1901 and made his biggest profit ever up to that point. He made this profit by being patient, doing his own research, and letting his short profits run instead of taking a quick gain when his trade proved correct. He also would not listen to others who said he was on the wrong side of the market and that stock at the time. In June of 1901, the price had risen to $130 per share. Through his research, he thought the high price would not be sustained due to the fact that copper conditions didn't look to support the price of the stock.

In July and August of that year, the price indeed began to decline. On September 6, 1901 President McKinley was shot in an attempted assassination attempt and went into a coma. Baruch decided to start shorting the stock, due to the uncertainty of the country and events at the time. He stayed fast to his thinking that the supply of copper would exceed the demand. He continued to short the stock on its decline, as his original positions were proving him right. When he closed his positions near $60 per share, he netted nearly $700,000 in profit. This transaction also gave him confidence in his ability to stick to his research and the facts.

Shortly thereafter he began purchasing Louisville & Nashville Railroad (L&N) after studying the company and their prospects for profits.

The price was at under $100 per share during the summer of 1901 after the sharp decline of Northern Pacific, which had previously run up significantly, and its subsequent decline was partly responsible for causing the panic of 1901. He began purchasing L&N because of his studies, and he wanted to realize one of his boyhood dreams of owning and running a railroad. By January 1902, L&N was in a strong uptrend. With a group of investors he began buying more shares in trying to gain control of the company. His dream never materialized, as his group never gained full control of the company, but he ended up selling his shares at a considerable profit of nearly $1 million.

By the age of 32, after five years of experience on Wall Street, Baruch had accumulated $3.2 million in wealth and was gaining a strong reputation on Wall Street as a successful speculator. In the summer of 1902, he cashed out of the market and traveled to Europe to contemplate his future of either staying in Wall Street or pursuing a law or medical degree and career, which were two areas of study he had always considered. He decided to stay in Wall Street due to his successes, and in August of 1903, at the age of 33, he retired from the firm of A.A. Housman & Company to trade exclusively on his own, as he found it crucial to his success to play a lone hand.

What he actually discovered was that he traded less and paid less attention to the minor daily fluctuations of the market and started concentrating more time in constructive enterprises and investments in certain companies and industries. This is where he would begin to succeed in ventures that would earn him a reputation as a skilled financier, as well as a successful stock speculator.

The Birth of a Speculator

One example of how he succeeded was when he began looking for new opportunities and started studying rubber companies, due to the increasing popularity of the automobile at the time. He began purchasing shares of Rubber Goods Manufacturing during the Rich Man's Panic (as it was so called) of 1903. He then would look for other industries that would benefit if one strong product group was favorable at the time. This purchase of Rubber Goods Manufacturing led him to own, and form with other investors, the Continental Rubber Company, which eventually became known as Intercontinental Rubber Company. He eventually sold out his position for a substantial profit.

In early 1904, Baruch heard that the Soo Line was planning on increasing its wheat traffic by building a new rail line westward. He conducted extensive research and began buying at between $60 to $65 per share. Gossip began circulating that the line's potential would not be as great as originally thought. Baruch ignored this outside chatter. He was determined not to be deterred by outside influences and opinions, as he learned this lesson a few years before. A bumper crop of wheat came along, revenue for the Soo Line increased 50 percent, and the stock jumped to $110 per share. He furthered his study of the company, revisited its prospects, and found the results would not support the increased price in the stock. He then sold his shares before the stock broke.

Baruch attributed this profitable transaction to superior research and study and his increasing experience in understanding the price actions of stocks. It pays to be able to change your views and not become emotionally embedded in one direction (bullish or bearish) or another when it comes to stocks. This transaction proved how through study and research Baruch would take action based on what he believed to be the facts. His swift change of direction, when he thought the conditions changed, were key reasons why he was successful with the Soo Line transaction.

Success and Power

By the age of 35, Baruch was an established speculator and millionaire, and he was building a reputation as a successful financier. He became incredibly wealthy at a young age by learning not to repeat the mistakes of his early years and through hard work, constant research, and study.

Baruch was unaffected by the crash of 1907 by staying attuned to the action of the market, and in fact, even contributed $2 million during the crash. He donated $1.5 million to the Bank of Manhattan Company to assist in the liquidity crisis that the crash had caused, and he also lent $500,000 to the Utah Copper Company so they could meet their payroll needs and not disrupt their business operations.

His dealings on Wall Street gave him an intimate knowledge of the personal character of many of the business leaders he had to deal with during his later endeavors during wartime. His Wall Street experience served him well in all his endeavors and in life in general. Baruch's father was a prominent physician and a large influence on Bernard's life, and he had been thinking of leaving Wall Street in pursuit of more noble causes as opposed to just making money trading in stocks.

Through his many contacts as a successful businessman, Baruch left Wall Street and went into public service as World War I broke out. He served as chairman of the War Industries Board and was called by President Woodrow Wilson to Paris to assist in drafting the peace treaty. When he was asked to serve on the War Industries Board by President Wilson, Baruch sold his seat on the exchange and all shares he held in companies that could possibly benefit from any government contracts in order to avoid any conflicts of interest.

Following his public service duties after World War I, he discovered public service more satisfying than just trading stocks and making money. The experience he gained from World War I changed his thinking. He became a member of the Advisory Commission of the Council of National Defense. His responsibilities were to see that raw materials would be available for the United States preparedness program. He later also worked in public service under the administration of President Theodore Roosevelt. His reputation earned him the ability to serve as a counselor to many of those in power. He actually held appointive positions in four Administrations, and he served as an advisor to six different presidents. One of his other high-ranking posts was that of the head of the American delegation to the United Nations Atomic Energy Commission in 1946.

Though he was said to have left trading on Wall Street when he entered public service, he actually kept his attention to the market by observing it and trading, though it would not consume his full-time attention. It seems the balance of trading in stocks and serving his country was something that satisfied him. He still was a rather large participant in the markets by most standards, as his trading records show his winning positions in 1925 (a strong year for the stock market) producing more than $1.4 million and his losing trades amounting to a little more than $415,000. Notice how he kept his losing trades to a manageable level when compared to his gains. In the choppy market of 1926, he managed a net profit of more than $457,000.

In 1928, as the market was shooting straight up, Baruch moved his offices closer to Wall Street. He was very bullish concerning the business climate in the United States during the mid- to late 1920s. As increased speculation was widespread and growing throughout 1928 and 1929 and prices were rapidly rising, Baruch was very active in the market. He was, by his own account, mostly out of the market before the crash, noting that he had become uncomfortable with the almost uninterrupted rise of stock prices. It is said that he saw the top of the market coming in October 1929, though some of his records do show he was still buying stocks during and throughout October of that year, even after the first major sharp breaks in the market had occurred. His records for 1929 did show a trading profit for the year of more than $615,000 (though this would not have reflected stocks he had not yet sold as of the end of that year).

After the first big breaks in the market, Baruch seemed more confident that the worst was over and mentioned to many that the financial storm had passed, as he kept to his bullish outlooks on American business. Reality of course was that the worst was far from over and depression periods would linger for some time. It is estimated that at the market's top in 1929, Baruch's net worth was somewhere near $25 million. He did, however, not seem to be too terribly impacted by the major decline in the market from late 1929 to the middle of 1932, when the market finally bottomed at 41.22 on July 8th (the market peaked on September 3, 1929 at 381.17). This can be supported by the fact that his lifestyle had not changed much, as he continued vacationing and donating to political causes, etc.

Even in the mid-1950s, Baruch (then in his eighties) was said to have spent time on the phone with his brokers, placing trades here and there for 10,000 shares at a time and watching the tape for hours. He would still be called upon by many to give his assessment of the current market. He would usually respond by saying that nobody could predict the stock market and that he certainly was not going to try.

Throughout his career, Baruch was very good at managing the personal fortune he attained, and during the late 1940s he began giving generously to universities and medical institutions in honor of his father's medical career and commitments to the medical profession. These donations were made to further the research and advance of the study of physical medicine. His incredible financial success also allowed him to purchase the famous Hobcaw property in South Carolina. He owned 17,000 acres, and many of his guests at the estate were U.S. presidents and other dignitaries. It is stated that the estate he left behind was valued at more than $14 million, and that he had given away to a variety of causes nearly $20 million over his lifetime.

Baruch wrote about his life with the publication of his book *My Own Story*, which published in 1957 and became an instant bestseller. He lived a full, satisfying, and rewarding life and died in 1965 at the age of 94.

The Baruch Approach

Baruch took an intelligent approach to the market. One of the skills he believed is a requirement to be honest with yourself and expect to be wrong as many times as you are right. He is often quoted saying "No speculator can be right all the time. In fact, if a speculator is correct half of the time, he is hitting a good average. Even being right three or four times out of ten should yield a person a fortune if he has the sense to cut his losses quickly on the ventures where he has been wrong."

He also talked about selling to the "sleeping point" as someone once told him. This means selling stocks if they keep you awake at night worrying about them. You need to use your subconscious mind to tell you to sell so you stop needlessly worrying.

Do Your Homework and Get the Facts

Baruch also believed, as did Livermore, that the way to truly succeed in the market was to devote oneself full time to the task. Because of the extreme challenge, one must commit full attention to it. He viewed it as no different than trying to be a successful doctor or lawyer. You simply must devote yourself full time to the study of your craft. The market, like any worthwhile pursuit, required an extreme amount of vigilance.

He thought that the stock market did not determine the health of the economy but rather that it reflects it. The ability to understand this and react to it is a must skill. He believed that stock prices reflect the economic facts and that overoptimism, as reflected in bullish high prices, is even more dangerous than pessimism because caution is ignored. This he experienced firsthand during the mid- to late 1920s. This means that bears are as significant as bulls in an efficient market because they restrain the extreme optimism and provide a balance to the market. The skill here is knowing in which environment you are participating. For Baruch, as was the case with Livermore, he would trade both sides of the market, depending on the conditions at the time. This flexible approach served him well, as he would profit from both being long and short.

Baruch discovered through experience that it is an essential skill for the successful speculator to be able to react quickly to the changes the market constantly produces. This proved meaningful when he learned how a bull market could break quickly once the continuity of thought behind the current market trend is broken. He believed that there is no sure investment and that one could not count on an investment to be absolute and unchanging. For this, the speculator needs to be reactionary, as the market is constantly changing.

This has been repeated throughout history in the market. The stock market basically reflects the current economic activity and the expectations for future economic activity. Therefore it is crucial to stay attuned to changes in industries and companies that either create new industries or improve on existing industries.

For example, in 1898 the market had 60 percent of its issues on the big board in the railroad industry. By 1914, this declined to 40 percent. In 1925, it declined further to 17 percent and by 1957, railroads consisted of only 13 percent of all stocks. Fast forward to today and railroads of course consist of only a handful of issues and represent a very small minority of all stocks listed on the exchanges.

Today's stocks consist of many different innovative industries such as biotechnology, semiconductors, electronics, and many other leading technology industries. This proves the market always changes and adapts to new ideas and innovations. The shrewdest traders throughout history all adapted the skill of reactionary change, as the market constantly presents new and different opportunities.

Baruch believed that people behave according to the curious psychology of crowds. As said by J.P. Morgan, the "continuity of thought" concerns how crowds react to events. Education and status provide no advantages during these events. These crowds' reactions caused the frenzy of the rising prices of the late 1920s, which eventually led to The Great Crash. So it doesn't really matter how high your IQ might be or what status you might have attained in some other profession, the market reacts indifferently to participants and doesn't really care who you might be as an individual. This understanding of psychology and its impact on the market was a key discovery for Baruch in his quest for profits.

Baruch also understood that what drives the prices of stocks is the human reactions to the economic forces and changing events presented and anticipated. The key to successful stock trading is the ability to separate ourselves from our own emotions. Baruch struggled with this also, as most traders do, but eventually he learned how to control the emotional aspects through his experience and trading rules. Without control over your emotions, there is very little chance for profitable success in the stock market.

Bernard Baruch described the stock market as the thermometer and the economic environment as the fever. The market does not cause economic cycles but merely reflects them and the judgments of what traders believe business and the future will be like. He believed the keys to the strength of economic conditions were a strong national defense and a strong national credit. The ability to understand the relationship between the market and the economy and how the market really works is a required skill for survival and success in the market.

He was a firm believer in judgment and thought. Baruch believed that information without judgment and thought was of little value. And he felt that in order to have good judgment one must have the big picture in focus. He also likened alertness and the ability to make non-biased judgments as keys to success in the stock market.

His views on determining the reasons why so many people lose money in the market is that they think they can make money by not working for it. He believed that most people view the market as the place where the miracle of great and quick riches can be performed with little effort. However, he proved that the market is not a place to expect riches without the required sacrifice that the market demands. When the market did provide profits for him, he made sure to become more humble as the market kept going his way. This pliable trait provided a balance for him so he would act in a prudent manner when it came to making the right trading decisions.

Custom-Made Discipline

Baruch became disciplined in his approach to the market after early experiences produced many losses. His number-one discipline was to never buy on tips or inside information. Relying on that kind of information produced some early losses for him, including a major loss on American Spirits. From that point on, he was sure to rely only on the cold, hard facts. He was a firm believer in doing your own research and finding out everything you can about the company, its management, its competition, its earnings, and its future growth possibilities. Self-reliance and doing one's own thinking was a must.

Baruch believed that you simply must get the facts of a situation before you act and commit hard-earned money to a transaction. He warned to always be on the lookout for tips from even the least-expected so-called stock experts. He recalled once in late 1929 a beggar to whom he would give gratuities to on a regular basis, telling him one day that he had a stock tip for Baruch to act upon. This event is similar to one often associated with Joseph P. Kennedy, a very successful stock speculator during the 1920s and father to former President John F. Kennedy. Joseph P. Kennedy mentioned that at one time during the great rising market of 1929, before the crash, a shoe shine boy had offered to give him a stock tip. Kennedy was sure that the market must have been near a top if shoe shine boys had become stock market experts by offering buying tips. The thinking here is that if everyone is invested in the market there is no more room for upward rising prices if all the demand has been met. Of course the events of the beggar offering advice to Baruch and the shoe shine boy offering tips to Kennedy happened to occur right before the Great Crash of 1929. Both Baruch and Kennedy had liquidated many of their positions before the crash devastated most portfolios.

Baruch did not believe that one needed to diversify too much, but that it was better to have a few stocks and to watch them carefully. He thought that one could simply not know all the relevant facts concerning too many stocks at one time. Focus was also a key skill he discovered that led to his success in the market. He believed that traders should focus on one thing at a time. He thought no one could be an expert at too many things. He liked to focus on one thing at a time, perfect it, and do it well.

Like Livermore, Baruch would do an analysis of all his trades to see if there were changes that needed to be made in his approach to the market. He also used this analysis to discover mistakes he had made so he could avoid making those same mistakes in the future. He started this early in his trading career. To do a thorough analysis and not become distracted, Baruch believed in removing himself as far away from the market as he could at times. This would mean leaving New York for getaways and liquidating his positions when necessary. He would actually take annual European vacations each summer. It is often mentally healthy to totally escape the activities of the market and use this down time to reflect on one's past transactions. Livermore also discovered how valuable this time away from the market was to him, as he would take many vacations to escape and recharge himself for his return to the markets. For Baruch, this time away was important so he could have the peace of mind and concentration to reflect on his transactions.

One discipline Baruch learned early after his mistake in American Spirits was to never invest all your funds, but to keep a good supply of cash on hand in a reserve. He did this to avoid betting his entire stake and going broke when things went against him. He also wanted a cash reserve, especially at the bottoms of market declines, so he could benefit from the eventual rise in the market that he knew would always come. This capital reserve would then be available for him to take advantage of those new opportunities.

Baruch knew the rewards of hard work, and he disciplined himself to the task at hand. He knew it required hard work to get the right information in order to make intelligent trades. The market demands vigilance, and he applied his efforts to his greatest abilities.

Learning from experience, he found it best to keep silent about his positions and trades, and he believed it was best to trade alone. When he decided to retire from A.A. Housman & Company and go out on his own, Baruch did so because he thought it was best to trade alone and remain focused in order to achieve the greatest profits.

He found through his years of trading that the two main mistakes that contributed to his early losses were the same mistakes he believed that most investors make, which were:

- They know too little about the company's management, earnings, prospects, and possibility for future growth.
- They tend to trade beyond their financial capital capacity.

These were the mistakes he made that caused him to lose his entire capital many times. He vowed to discipline himself to learn from these, and that was one of the reasons he became so committed to the extensive research he would conduct on the companies he was interested in investing in.

Baruch's understanding of financial statistics lent quite a bit to the interpretation of the fundamentals of the companies he was studying. Today, we would say that Baruch was more of a fundamentalist type of trader than a technical trader. In evaluating the fundamentals and general qualities of a company, he would look at three main areas:

- The real assets of the company. Its cash and properties.
- That it must perform or produce something that is needed.
- That it must have good management.

He would discipline himself to check the company, especially its management, and the financial prospects before entering a trade.

Facts and Rules

Baruch was a disciplinarian who would research and stick to the facts rather than have a long list of trading rules. Of the trading rules he did develop and follow, however, he noted that cutting losses quickly was a must rule he learned through experience. Just as all the great traders in this book acknowledged, this was a crucial rule in protecting his capital and allowing him to accumulate his wealth throughout his lifetime.

When selling stocks, Baruch would many times sell his shares as the prices were rising, just as he did many times in 1929. He sold 121,000 shares of stock he held in the sulfur industry just before they peaked. By the time the crash occurred in October 1929, he was completely out of these holdings. One reason he retained his fortune was his ability to sell shares on the way up. He believed nobody could sell at the top and buy at the bottom. This "feel" he attained, especially after many years of experience, often caused him to sell when he felt prices rose too high. He did not seem to have specific rules of when prices were too high, but he developed more of a sense that one gets when they trade for many years and follow the market with intense study.

The other rules he followed came from mistakes that cost him in prior transactions. He made a mistake in 1906 when he entered the commodities market and bought coffee (which he did not know about—his first mistake), and as it started to drop in price he was told to hold on (another mistake——listening to others). He held on and watched it continue to drop. He made still another mistake by selling his other large holding at the time in Canadian Pacific stock, which had shown a growing profit. He sold these shares to raise more margin money for the coffee position. After he finally sold the losing position in coffee, he realized a loss of almost $700,000. Baruch reported feeling physically ill after this trade. He made a resolution to never trade in something he did not know about and to cut all his future losses short and to let his winners ride. He also realized how damaging something like that coffee experience could be to a trader's confidence.

Baruch always believed that it was much harder to sell stocks correctly than it was to buy them correctly. He noted that, because of the emotional aspect of trading, if a stock went up, the average investor would hold because he wants more gains—he's exhibiting greed. If the stock declines, he also holds on and hopes the stock will come back so he can at least sell and break even—he's hoping against hope. Baruch worked hard to avoid the impact these emotions can play on a trader, which can be very damaging. His rules were to sell stocks on the way up, and if the stock was declining, he would quickly sell and realize his loss.

He sold several times in 1928 as the market was climbing to record highs. As stocks kept rising he would come right back into the market and purchase more. This trading behavior proves how important it is to follow what the market is currently doing as opposed to following what one might personally think the market should do. By August 1929, the market was rising so fast that Baruch would buy stocks on strength one day and then sell them the next day. His trading rules were letting his judgment and the actions of the market dictate to him what actions he should take.

Carefully following the strategies he implemented during his career and being disciplined in his trading allowed Baruch to become a very wealthy and important figure in the business world, and then to realize personal satisfaction in serving his country and being a trusted advisor to several U.S. presidents.

3

GERALD M. LOEB

"What everybody else knows is not worth knowing."

The Skittish Trader

Born in 1899, Gerald M. Loeb started investing in 1921 when he was working in the bond department for a brokerage firm in San Francisco. He did not take to sales very much, and he started reading everything he could on speculation, investing, money, real estate, and economics. He started investing with an inheritance of $13,000 from his father as his capital account. As his interest in stock trading began to grow, he found he also liked writing and wrote some briefs concerning financial statistics and bonds that were published in late 1921.

In 1923, Loeb took a substantial loss in proportion to his capital, and just like the other traders we've profiled he used that lesson to help him become more successful by learning from his mistakes. He then landed a position as a stockbroker with E.F. Hutton & Co. and moved to New York in 1924, where he stayed, eventually became a partner, and later vice-chairman of the board after it was incorporated in 1962.

He made a name for himself as a newspaper columnist and market writer, as articles he had published were featured in *Barron's, The Wall Street Journal,* and *Investor Magazine.* In 1935, Loeb wrote his popular book *The Battle for Investment Survival.* The book sold more than 200,000 copies in its first printing, and due to reader demand was updated in 1957. In 1965, Loeb again updated the book with additional information, though practically no changes were made to the basic strategies that first appeared in the 1935 original.

When *The Battle for Investment Survival* originally was due to hit the bookshelves, another popular investment book was also coming out. Benjamin Graham's *Security Analysis* has been considered the bible for the buy-and-hold investor, as Graham was deemed the father of value investing.

Graham and Loeb couldn't have come at the market from more opposite approaches. These two differing styles had contrasting opinions as to which way of investing in the market was the more prudent and profitable. Though there have been many successful value investors over the years, the most famous of course being Warren Buffett, Loeb himself amassed millions in the stock market during his lifetime.

While Buffett is viewed by many as more of a long-term investor, due to his style of investing in stocks and companies and holding them for many years, Loeb viewed the stock market as more of a battlefield. He believed that the battle for profits was far too risky to hold stocks for long periods of time, as the title to his famous book depicts. This view came about over the many years he was investing, as he witnessed the Crash of 1929 firsthand. The events of the Crash proved to him that holding onto stocks, and ignoring the sell side, can have a devastating effect on one's portfolio.

Loeb, by his own account, was mostly out of the market before the Crash. An astute trader, Loeb had discovered that the top of the 1929 market actually occurred on September 3rd, almost a full two months before the beginning of The Great Crash. The experience of the Great Crash made Loeb a skittish trader for the remainder of his career, as opposed to a long-term investor. In fact, Loeb wrote a follow-up book titled *The Battle for Stock Market Profits* in 1971; published some 36 years after the publication of his first book, he still viewed the market as a battlefield.

His style consisted of taking advantage of trends in the marketplace, buying and selling at key points, taking quick profits, and cutting his losses short. He thought that most people give the market no thought or study, or at least not the amount of effort it requires. Like Baruch, Loeb believed that most people look at the market as a way to gain quick riches. Loeb felt that this view was why most people fail at stock speculation, and his views matched the feelings that Livermore and Baruch had toward the psychology of investors. All three men believed that this naïve perception of the markets was what led to failure for most investors.

Loeb also believed that knowledge through experience is one trait that separates successful stock market speculators from everyone else. It was the experience that came to these great traders, who continuously learned from their failures, that ultimately paid great dividends down the road during their trading careers.

After more than 50 years in the investing battlefield and the success and wealth he accomplished during his life and career, Gerald Loeb definitely deserves the distinction to be labeled as one of the greatest. He withstood the test of time through many and varied market cycles. Unfortunately, his publications do not identify the specific trades where he made his fortunes, but nonetheless, he did detail the rules that contributed to his success.

Loeb's Keys

Loeb believed that the best stock market speculators need certain skills and knowledge to produce outstanding results. He believed in taking things more slowly and starting gradually. You need to assess your strengths and weaknesses, and this requires knowing yourself and your limitations, he noted.

Loeb, just like Livermore and Baruch before him, also defined speculation and distinguished between speculating and investing. He said that speculating is a careful study of the facts and reducing the risk by education and experience. As one gains more experience in the market, the value of that experience translates into knowledge, and the knowledge gained dictates what works and what does not work in the market. In the stock market, facts work, and the greatest traders know this.

Contemporaries in the markets, Loeb did get to know Bernard Baruch. Baruch who once wrote him stating, "After you have the facts, examine yourself as to whether you have prejudices or not, and then use your own judgment." Baruch, as mentioned earlier, used the word speculator because he felt there was no sure investment. To him, application and diligence were the keys to success. As for Loeb, he decided that if you want to accumulate capital you must speculate and not invest. Investing was putting your money away and getting a return. Speculating was taking a calculated risk based on an intelligent estimate of future possibilities. He also thought that with a great deal of understanding, observation, and study, one could be very successful not by merely buying a good fundamental stock and holding it forever, but rather by staying attuned to the market changes and taking advantage of those changes.

Quickness and Discipline Pay Off

Loeb believed that short-term trading (holding a stock between 6 months and 18 months) was much more profitable than long-term investing because it would force you into the right stocks at the right time. Loeb thought it nearly impossible for someone to predict what the market was going to do at a point well into the future. Like the weather, it was easier to predict what might happen tomorrow or the next day as opposed to many months down the road. This take on the market caused Loeb to become a skittish trader. He would dart in and out of stocks as the market dictated.

The changing elements of the market were also very important to Loeb, as the earlier the change in the trend was detected, the more profits could be realized if you observed and acted appropriately to take advantage of those changes in trends. Because the market is really reflecting the supply and demand of investor expectations, and many participants might have differing views on those expectations, changes in price trends will always occur. It's the ability to detect and act on the more meaningful changes, in the appropriate time frame, that can separate the really great profits from the mediocre profits.

Change was also a key skill to life as a speculator. The ability to change and seek out changes will greatly enhance your results, as stocks and market cycles change all the time, though they do seem to follow historical patterns. Though change is difficult for many people, it plays a crucial role in the life of a great stock trader. The ability to understand historical changes is also a vital skill, as the market has proven that certain patterns over time repeat themselves.

Loeb was a hard worker throughout his life, and he believed that hard work was a requirement to succeed in trading. He also believed that to do well in short-term trading, it took someone's full-time attention and dedication, just like Livermore and Baruch before him believed.

Loeb was a tape reader, similar to Livermore, and he believed that luck played no part in the success or failure of a trader. Rather, it is knowledge and a premium ability that lead to success. The amount of time devoted to understanding the markets would directly relate to your outcome. He thought that the market must be studied just like any other profession or endeavor. He believed that very few people would ever attain the highest success in stock trading, just like very few people ever attain the highest ranks in any other field, be it medicine, sports, music, science, or any other.

The best traits for successful speculation are knowledge, experience, and judgment. Loeb found that the best traders are usually psychologists and the worst performers are usually accountants. Accountants usually produce terrible trading results because of how they are trained. For example, accountants typically would put a certain value on a stock based on a certain P/E ratio or a certain book value. A certain (usually low) P/E ratio, they might concur, would indicate that the value of the stock might be low and should be considered as a possible buy candidate. But Loeb believed that the market really doesn't work in such a scientific way. Just because some set formula might indicate that a stock should be purchased doesn't necessarily mean the supply and demand that follow that purchase will reflect that value. As Loeb would show, this thinking can cost a trader serious profits. Loeb argued that you must trade with the actions of the market and not simply by how you might think the market should trade. You might think that certain low P/E ratio stocks should be bought due to a formula that rates them as undervalued in price, but the market might not think and behave in the same manner. If you purchase these stocks just because you adhere to a certain valuation formula and the market decides to value them differently after you purchase them, and you do not cut your losses short if the stocks decline in price, you could lose significant amounts of your capital if you still believe your formula should have been correct.

Loeb did not believe in paper trading, as he thought this removed the emotional part of investing, which is the most difficult part to overcome. You simply will not have the same emotional issues when you paper trade versus actually putting your hard-earned money on the line.

He noticed how psychological influences played a great part in setting market valuations. He showed how stocks would normally make new highs when the greatest number of people would visualize its greatest possible value, and not necessarily at the moment when the company's highest earnings or highest values are actually achieved. He, like those before him, thought emotions needed to be restrained and should play no part in trading decisions. Rather, trading decisions should be based on great opportunities—as opposed to hopeful situations and dreams. To take advantage of those situations, successful traders need to rely on solid trading rules instead of emotions.

He noticed that stocks, and companies for that matter, act like human beings. Stocks go through the same stages and phases as people do, including infancy, growth, maturity, and decline. The key in trading is to be able to recognize which stage the stock is in and to take advantage of that opportunity. This meant getting a deep understanding of the psychology of the market. The key place to be for the best profits is in the growth stage. Because people make prices and behind prices are profits, profits therefore are shaped by people. The actions of people and profits ultimately drive stock prices either up or down.

Because of the heavy human impact in the market, Loeb learned to stop being an analyst and became more of a psychologist. For example, every stock he owned in 1927 was based on fundamentals. Even though, through thorough analysis, he thought they were overvalued and then he sold them, these stocks kept moving up in price. Due to the continued rise in prices, he bought back in as the market was in a strong bullish stage. The psychology of the market was showing him that investors were in a buying frenzy and that classic analytical tools, if followed, would have kept one out of the market, due to historical valuation models not supporting the current high prices. This taught him how important it is to know how "excess" and "mob psychology" work, especially when it comes to the stock market. He also noticed how it didn't matter what he thought, as the market was going to come to its own conclusions concerning whether stocks were overvalued or undervalued.

Key qualities that Loeb felt were important for the successful trader to have in the complex environment of the market were:

- Intelligence
- Understanding of human psychology
- Flair based on pure objectivity
- Natural quickness
- Originality of thinking that remains logical

It was also important to understand your own thinking and to beware of the dangers that bull markets can do to your thinking, such as:

- Thinking you are smarter than the market
- Getting more aggressive in your approach

He found that great successes could lead to overconfidence, which would end up doing considerable damage if not contained. It is important to be confident, especially in the market, which looks uncertain most of the time. But Loeb felt it also was important to manage confidence levels to avoid getting out of control. This, of course, takes a great amount of discipline and self-control.

Also, great dangers can occur by not knowing at what stage or cycle the market is in. Most bull markets are recognized by the majority of investors and traders well after they have started. Most end when everyone is excited and overvaluation is considerable. Being able to actually know the exact stages of the market as they are occurring is crucial in being able to stay on top of the market and analyze its moves and direction as it's happening. This quickness is required in order to be ready to react to the direction of the market when it changes and to be one of the first to discover the change.

To trade successfully, Loeb knew that one must focus on price and volume action as key determining factors. After all, volume is the decisive determinant of demand, so it is crucial to show the balance and relationship between the two and how they interact.

To be one of the very best that truly succeed, Loeb believed you need to:

- Aim high—have ambitious goals.
- Control the risks.
- Be unafraid to keep uninvested reserves and be patient.

Loeb viewed the stock market as more of an art than a science. It is also very complex, as American and global economies are very complicated and involve many participants. This only supported his strong conviction that full-time attention and constant study are required to succeed in the market.

The best speculators know in their own right and have a rare art of understanding how to utilize and profit from their own knowledge and information from others. They have intuition and judgment that tells them when to actively participate and when to stand idle on the sidelines. They have a "feel" of when to be brave, when to retreat, when to add to rising positions, and when to cut losses shorter and shorter over time. They know when to be patient and impatient, when to be in and when to be out, and when to trust their judgment.

Discipline in Battle

Loeb believed that discipline is a very important requirement for achieving success over the long run in stock market trading. After all, the battlefield of investing requires strict adherence to sound disciplines.

One of Loeb's first and most important strategies was to understand and know the current general trend of the market. Once you have a good feeling for what stage the market is in, then you can proceed with rules for buying and selling stocks.

One of the widest differences between the successful investor and all others is the ability and discipline of the successful investor to be out of the market when it is not acting right instead of trying to constantly trade in a dangerous market. This takes considerable self-control, a vital asset to the successful trader. Many traders find out the hard way that overtrading, and especially trading against the market, is a losing strategy. Loeb thought it was better to do nothing in a bear market than to take a chance on doing something wrong. In a bull market the reverse is usually true. It can be a huge opportunity cost not to have cash ready to take advantage of the next upturn.

If markets were narrow and not showing clear signs and if the news were the determining factor, such as war, he would do nothing and sit on cash. If he did trade in those environments it would be in small amounts and transactions. It is important to have a cash reserve ready because it is difficult to know when the next upturn will come. Keeping a cash reserve and being out of the market keeps your confidence and emotions intact. Loeb would sit on cash for long periods of time just waiting for the right moment. He would also hold only a few particular stocks at any one time. This allowed him to focus on those issues and watch them very closely. His cash reserve was his ammunition for future buys. The cash reserve is a must for the successful speculator. It must always be ready and available for the next opportunity.

Loeb believed in concentration as opposed to diversification. He was a strong believer in not overdiversifying. He thought it was better to have a few concentrated stocks and watch them closely. "Put all your eggs in one basket and watch it very carefully," he often said. He thought that to diversify your assets over many types of investments and stocks would not produce the same results of concentrating, focusing, and knowing your stocks as well as you should.

This thinking went against all the other popular advice given in those days and still today. Loeb also believed that the more experienced and successful you become, the less you should diversify. He made all his money and success by concentrating on a few leaders of the day and watching their action very closely. This again is a hard discipline to implement, especially in a strong bull market when many stocks are racing up in price. But as Loeb's experience taught him, the big money was made in the leaders.

Loeb believed traders should set the return goals for themselves very high—for example trying to double their capital in 6 to 18 months. He believed that the very best speculators want to make a killing in the market. You simply must discipline your mind in setting goals at the highest levels. He believed that speculation is for large gains and not for "income" returns, but you need to measure and reduce the risk to as low as possible. This again relates to his strategy of holding or trading only a few stocks at any one time. This forces you to concentrate on a few issues that you know well and time your purchases at the minimum risk level.

Another key discipline, one that we saw in Livermore and Baruch and one we will see in Darvas and O'Neil as well, is the practice of evaluating your trades after the fact. Loeb would review his losing trades to keep himself learning and to avoid making those same mistakes in the future. Putting your spotlight and attention on your failures is a sure way to succeed. Understanding your mistakes is vital to trading success. Loeb would write down his reasons for making a trade before he made the trade. This would discipline him and move him away from impulse trades. He wrote down the pros and cons of a trade and how much he would expect to make beforehand. This also helped him in his selling. He believed that if you write down your reasons for buying, and then if the stock doesn't work out or changes later, that would be all you would need as a reason for selling. Lack of this disciplined proactive procedure is a large reason why so many traders fail. They simply ignore why they bought the stock in the first place, and they don't sell the stock when those reasons prove otherwise. He called this his "ruling reason." He created checklists to write down reasons why you should buy a stock. They would include:

- Fundamentals
- Valuations and trends (P/E ratios, historical growth rates, etc.)
- Objectives and risks
- General information

These reasons would help him to keep his emotions in check and discourage impulse buying, as he would discipline himself to just follow his reasoning rules.

Because Loeb believed that all securities are speculative and risky, he thought traders needed to be able to do their own analysis and make their own decisions. You should not listen to any other opinions or tips, but rely only on your own judgment. You need to be able to judge the action of the market cycle. And you need to be able to judge your own stocks within the context of the general market. You also need to be able to decide if the market is in an accumulation, distribution, or somewhere in the middle stage.

He believed that success in trading is measured in three dimensions:

- Risk
- Reward
- Consistency

The key was to control the risk and seek the highest returns with a consistency in your rules and strategies. As you learn from your mistakes, you will develop rules that will begin to work. It's important to refine and add to your rules as you find what works and what does not, but it's also important not to keep changing strategies for each and every different cycle. For example, it doesn't do any good to be a value investor one day and then a growth investor the next.

Loeb's selling rules included the basic premise that traders should always close a trade when a good reason exists to do so. This discipline usually separates short-term traders from long-term investors. Don't ignore sound market sell signals and hold on just because you think you're a long-term investor. This philosophy could be very costly (as we have seen since the dramatic bear market that began in the spring of 2000). Those investors who ignored the classic sell signals of the market and held on, or are still holding on, to fallen leaders have no doubt paid a huge price as the value of their portfolios has been reduced sharply over the past few years.

Loeb would also not sell stocks based solely on tax considerations. The more prudent and profitable way is to sell when the stock and/or the market gives signals to sell, and then pay the profits on the gains regardless if they become higher short-term capital gains or lower long-term capital gains. The key is to not let the change in the short- or long-term tax rate influence your sell decisions. He also thought stocks were the best hedge against inflation if they were purchased and sold at the correct times.

Because he was a tape reader, he thought that following the price movements were the key to stock action. The early stages of a market move are the best. Usually the strongest stocks will show strength before this occurs. That is why it is important to keep studying the market. These early movers will normally make new highs before the averages do and end up being the real leaders, providing the best price increases. He found that it was best to start worrying when stock prices are very high, when most investors are overly optimistic, and when everything in the market seems perfect. This was similar to what Livermore and Baruch believed, and it led them to do their selling into the strength while stock prices kept rising. Loeb also discarded the hype of P/E ratios as the prime measure for buying stocks, and he found they were rarely useful and presented, in general, an emotional reaction. He didn't give much credence to them as far as buying a stock, but he would analyze them, especially as stocks rose to high levels.

Another discipline Loeb believed in was advising traders to check the new high and new low lists. He thought that stocks that make new highs and quiet stocks that start to creep up in price and develop positive signs on higher volume were the best candidates for further study. This will automatically steer you to the new leaders to contemplate for new purchases. Get in the habit of scanning the stock tables looking for advances of one point or more on higher than normal volume. These are the stocks that are showing developing strength.

Loeb's many disciplines allowed him to ride through the 1929–1932 bear market, making money every year. He was a strict disciplinarian, and it was one of the biggest reasons why he avoided many losses and produced incredible gains.

Rules of the Perfect Trade

Loeb perfected his trading rules over the more than 50 years of his trading career. He used margin when he was young and encouraged using it during the younger years of a trader's career.

His first trading rule for success is the ability to accept losses, cut them short, and move on if the stock moves against you. This was his insurance policy to protect against large losses. Just like Livermore and Baruch before him, his rule was to limit his losses to no more than 10 percent. This was his absolute maximum and a rule that he could simply not ignore. This is the one vital rule that should be automatic and act as a substitute for any emotions that always will come into play when a trade goes against you.

William J. O'Neil even mentions in his book, *How to Make Money in Stocks,* that he had the opportunity to meet Loeb when he was writing his book *The Battle for Stock Market Profits.* Loeb told O'Neil that he hoped to be out of a trade long before it ever dropped to 10 percent from his purchase price.

The benefit of experience will give the best traders a sense of when a stock is not acting properly before it ever gets to their stated loss-cutting rule. You simply must be able to take your losses quickly in the battlefield of stock trading to survive and prosper. Loeb would repeat this rule over and over again in his publications as he constantly stressed its importance in the arsenal of the successful trader.

Another important rule is to monitor the general trend of the market. The trend of the market is so important that it also determines how certain other trading rules are implemented and acted upon. When the market was heading up (as in the early stages of an advance or just when the market was emerging from a weak environment), Loeb would look for the active leaders and buy into them. He believed you should buy only quality stocks if the trend is up, and you should limit your buys to the leaders of the strongest industry groups.

Volume also was a vital signal and key trait. Strong up days on strong volume is very bullish. Decreasing volume on up days in price is a bearish sign (up to a point). He would constantly stay observant and use his experience. Though Loeb was not a technical chartist, he was a tape reader of price action.

In a bull market it is always wise to pay up for an active leader. Loeb also looked for new highs crossing a resistance level with correct timing of an upward-trending market. This was the exact same strategy that Livermore was discovering in his trading experiences.

Loeb also liked it when the major moves above these certain levels in price were accompanied by large increases in volume. This again confirmed the demand for the stock. This is why he believed in watching the price movement of stocks. He believed that institutional holding and buying of certain stocks was an important element of a successful stock and positive for future profits. He also looked for relative strength in the leaders when the market makes a turn from a correction or reaction. This is a key trait in helping to identify future leaders and proves the strength and conviction that investors have in the stock.

The best stocks to buy and how much to buy is dictated by the action of the general market. The best buy signal is when a stock moves up strongly on larger volume and the stock is breaking out of accumulation stages. Loeb favored higher stock prices as they usually kept rising, were the active leaders that could lead to big price gains, and had a strong following. The best stocks will always seem overpriced to the majority of investors. He avoided the cheap stocks, as they usually got cheaper. Low-priced stocks, he learned through his trading, reflect bad value as opposed to a bargain value. Again, this philosophy went against most opinions in the market in Loeb's days.

Loeb also noticed that every new market cycle produces a new list of fresh leaders. It was unusual for the former leaders to become the standouts during the next rising market cycle. At the tops of market cycles, the main area of concentration and focus should be on trend and action, as those will then dictate the price action and will produce the new leaders.

Loeb, just like Livermore and Baruch, believed that smart traders would pyramid their buys on new highs. This was akin to the probing and pyramiding strategy Livermore introduced many years before. Loeb would pyramid up in increments to test if his buys were correct. For example, if he decided to trade 1000 shares in a particular issue, as he would always decide beforehand the total number of shares he was going to invest in each particular stock, he would buy 100 shares on his initial purchase. Then, if the stock moved up as he anticipated, he would purchase another 200 shares. He would then add more shares to his purchases as the stock kept moving in the proper direction. He kept on averaging up to his initial level of 1000 shares if the stock was doing well and was still within the correct buying range. Again, all the great traders featured in this book used this strategy as a key rule for attaining large profits.

Loeb also believed that stocks are always way overvalued in a bull market and way undervalued in a bear market. He was guided more by trend in the market than by price. He noticed through experience that the reason why low or high points are made will be revealed many months later. It is the expectation, not the news itself, that moves the market. This is why it is crucial to understand the time element of news and the price adjustment reactions to news. The price reactions usually never happen at exactly the same time. He noticed many times that market prices are usually also ahead of the general news, business, and corporate developments. War is a good example of this. He considered war or the threat of war as the greatest hazard for the investor. It tended to cause the most uncertainty.

Loeb stuck to his sound principles and believed that a good tape reader depends only on buys because of good action in the stock. He never traded on news alone, as he used it to consider its relation to the tape action and not to the stock itself.

Loeb basically stuck to three basic elements in appraising the worth of a stock to see if it was in a good position for purchase. They were:

- Quality—good fundamentals, liquidity, and good management
- Price—based on the rules presented earlier
- Trend—the most important element and easier to detect than price

The trend is the most important quality, especially in the early and middle stages of a higher trending advance.

One of the main fundamental traits that Loeb liked in a stock was good management at a company, and top managers also had to have a solid ownership stake in the company. He thought that the dominant mover of stocks was the earnings of the company and the expectation of increased future earnings. He believed that this was the main mover of a stock's price from the fundamental side.

As far as money management rules, Loeb would follow these, which he found to be sound over his many years in the market.

- Strive for ultimate gains of 1 ½ to 2 times your capital in 6 to 18 months.
- Professionals risk a maximum of 20 percent of their capital on one issue.
- It is more advantageous to invest in an advancing issue at seemingly higher prices than to attempt to discover when the bottom will turn up for a particular issue. To the best traders "the most expensive is actually the cheapest."

Loeb didn't have many sell rules when he was ahead on profitable positions, as he relied more on his experience and his judgment. One of his favorite times to sell was when he started patting himself on the back for being so clever and outsmarting the market. This is almost always a huge mistake, and one you should be aware of. This overconfidence has been detrimental to many a stock trader over the years. When you start bragging about how great you are, the market seems to have a magical way of bringing you back down to earth in a humbling manner.

He noticed that tops in stocks would usually occur when the advance in price stalls as volume or activity increases, or if the prices decline and the activity increases. This again comes from the focus and constant observation of the market and your holdings.

Loeb thought that the age and extent of an advance was an important element and factor in his sell decisions. He would intend to sell his leaders that had been there for two or three years first versus the ones that had just begun to move. He believed there were exhaustion points in leaders that had advanced a great deal over that period of time. Remember, Loeb was a short-term and skittish trader, so it would not have been unusual for him to think in those terms.

Some sell guidelines he adhered to when he was in a bull market were:

- Sell when you see a bear market ahead (in bear markets he would go to 100-percent cash)

- Sell when you see trouble for your particular company
- Sell when time has offered a far better buy (weed yourself of laggards in your portfolio and move on to new leaders)

He always believed that if your stock stops going up and begins to decline, you should always sell your worst shares first and keep your best performers in your portfolio. One strategy Loeb always advocated was to sell approximately 10 percent of his portfolio at the end of each year. This rule would force him to weed his portfolio of the weakest stocks and move his money into stronger positions if they presented themselves, keeping the best performers and removing the stale stocks.

Some other sell signals he would look for was when the stock rose sharply on big volume but ended the day at no gain or at a loss. This indicated a reversal of the earlier strength in the stock and signaled a possible waning of the strong demand for the stock. For example, Loeb saw the top in the Crash of 1929 as the leaders started to act badly. When he moved out of them, forced out by their nonperformance and into other stocks, and they to started to act badly, he noticed there was nothing else strong to buy. The market action automatically kicked him out of his positions and told him there was nothing desirable left to buy by its action. Also, he began to take his profits as they began to diminish. He believed that selling was much harder to do than buying, and the successful selling of stocks is what separated the men from the boys. The key to selling is to be able to sell into the strength of the stocks that you already own and show a substantial profit. You need to sell before it's obvious to everyone else. This takes extreme discipline and is a main trait of all those featured in this book.

The main selling rules that Loeb employed were basically the two listed below:

- Cut your losses short at no more than 10 percent.
- Prune your portfolio 10 percent at a minimum at year end. Sell your worst 10-percent positions to weed out the weakness in your portfolio.

All other decisions he made when it came to selling were either based on guidelines or were made on judgment. He learned through his many years that the more experience you gain, the better your judgment will become.

Loeb believed that every stock will have periods when it will be the opportune time to buy and when it will be a good time to sell. The selective buying and selling, and the ability to spot these different times, is the key to the most profitable opportunities and is usually a main reason why some profit and most lose in the market.

He identified three main reasons why many tend to lose money in the market:

- Paid too much (not paying attention to the technical side)
- Did not recognize a bad balance sheet (loss of focus of the fundamentals)
- Misled by inaccurate earnings estimates (another fundamental item)

Another possible reason for selling is if a stock is going up rapidly and becomes overvalued and splits because of its high price. This would be a strong signal for him, as he noticed many times that this action would lead to price declines.

As for shorting, Loeb found it to be rarely successful (usually because most bear markets are less severe in nature than rising or bull markets), but if you do want to try shorting stocks, he advised following these guidelines:

- Anticipate bad news (which is very hard to do most of the time)
- Watch for unfavorable relative action such as breaking certain trend lines, failures on rallies, and a downward overall trend in the market

He also advised to never short a stock because you feel it is too high priced. It is better to let the action of the market determine if the stock is too high priced rather than your own personal opinion. The fundamentals of the company should be weakening and the stock should be making new lows before you consider shorting a stock.

Gerald Loeb detailed all of his skills, disciplines, and trading rules in the two books he wrote on the stock market. His many years and successes in the stock market are truly remarkable feats and should be studied by every aspiring trader who wants to become one of the best.

4

Nicolas Darvas

"As for good stocks and bad stocks, there were no such things; there were only stocks increasing in price and stocks declining in price."

The Persistent "Outsider"

Nicolas Darvas is the only one of *The Greatest Stock Traders of All Time* profiled in this book that did not start or even have a career in the brokerage business. Darvas was born in 1920 in Hungary. He studied economics at the University of Budapest and fled to Turkey during World War II. He came to the United States in 1951 and was part of an international professional dance team (Darvas and Julia), when in November of 1952, he was offered to be paid in stock instead of cash from one of the nightclubs his team was going to perform at in Toronto.

The stock was a small Canadian mining penny stock called Brilund. At the time, Darvas knew basically nothing about stocks. He was offered 6000 shares, which were valued at 50 cents a share at the time, as compensation for his services. He actually ended up not being able to make the performance, but out of courtesy he offered to buy the stock anyway.

After the purchase, he thought nothing of the stock until he checked the price for the first time two months later. Much to his amazement the stock had appreciated in value to $1.90 per share. He could hardly believe what he saw, and he immediately sold the stock and netted a profit of nearly $8000. He was so amazed at the profit potential of this transaction that he became totally hooked on the stock market.

From this first profitable experience, Darvas became fascinated with and took a strong interest in learning more about stocks. As with most people who decide to give stock trading a try, Darvas followed the typical pattern, looking for the "secret" to the market. Because he had no experience in the stock market, he really didn't know where to start and what to do. So he started asking people he knew and came into contact with during his daily affairs to see if they knew of any good stocks and if they had any good tips. As he soon found out, most people he talked to seemed to know quite a bit about stocks and were more than willing to give him their advice about what stocks to buy. Many people would give him names of stocks that would certainly make him a rich man in a short period of time. He kept these first buys and tips confined to Canadian penny stocks—after all, that was where he realized this first great profit—so there had to be more to come from these great little gems.

This haphazard system, like so many usually discover, produced dismal results and soon he was averaging approximately $100 a week in losses. It seemed like all the eager advice that came his way did not amount to much success. He would trade by moving in and out of stocks very quickly, usually trading more as he would receive additional tips. He would sometimes hold 25 to 30 different stocks at one time, and the ones that did well for him he liked so much he would call them his "pets." He even started trading to the old saying "you can never go broke by taking a profit," and this caused him to take very small profits when he had them, which led to overtrading. After nearly a year had passed, he started becoming disgruntled that the next Brilund had not come along, so he decided to change strategies.

Darvas then began to subscribe to stock market newsletters and investment subscription services. After all, the writers of these newsletters and services had to be the experts, as they followed the market constantly. This made much more sense to him than listening to the average person on the street. He began blindly buying the recommendations that were featured in the newsletters. Once again, the results he desired were not to be had, and not only was he losing more money in the market, but it was also costly to continue the subscription services.

Next, Darvas decided he would go right to the best sources, the brokers. After all, they were not only in the market every day, they actually earned their living by advising people on what stocks to buy. With a broker, Darvas was now going to trade in stocks listed on the New York Stock Exchange, and he thought he now had discovered the secret of the market. After all, now he was a real player in the big market. He was trading about once a day and thought he had become a true stock operator. To better understand the language of his broker and the street, he began to read all the books he could on the stock market and investments. Darvas mentions in a feature article in *Time* magazine that he read over 200 books on the stock market and great speculators.

After the knowledge gained from reading all about the market and finance, he decided to concentrate more on the fundamentals of stocks because the advice he was getting from his broker was not producing very positive results. This focus on the fundamentals required a great deal of attention to detail and careful analysis. He studied this extensively. Along the way he studied annual reports, insider trading, and began to do other types of research. He started to base his trades on certain popular Wall Street favored statistics such as P/E ratios, stock ratings, etc. These trades also did not produce very positive results, but it was here that he started to discover that industry groups were important, and that there was a certain follow-the-leader style to the market. He would then decide to select the most active and strongest group and choose the leader, based strictly on fundamentals, of that group.

From this analysis he discovered a stock called Jones & Laughlin Steel, of which the steel group had been a market leader at the time. He bought 1000 shares on margin (which at the time was 70 percent) at the price of $52.50 per share. He put $36,750 into this stock, which was all the money he had. He could not believe his eyes as the price started to fall, despite all the study he did on the fundamentals and how he carefully selected this leading stock. He simply would not accept the fact that the price was declining, and he kept thinking that this stock did not support a fall in its price. As the price fell further, he finally sold at $44 per share. He had lost approximately $9000.

While the Jones & Laughlin Steel experience was a devastating blow to his newfound strategy, he noticed while searching through the paper a stock called Texas Gulf Producing. This stock kept rising in price even though he had not heard of this company. He didn't quite know why the price kept rising; all he knew was that it was rising. He could not believe the rise in this stock, as he was certain that he would have come across this company when he was doing his research of superior fundamental stocks. After following the stock and its price behavior, he decided to buy 1000 shares at $37.25 per share and subsequently sold five weeks later at $43.25 a share for a $5000 profit after commissions.

Nearly three years had passed since the profitable Brilund transaction, and after trying the many trading methods we mentioned previously, Darvas learned from this trade that the reason why the stock was going up in price was because of the action of the stock within the market itself, and that is what he decided was what really mattered.

He then decided to act on the actions of the market itself and began to carefully study the price action among stocks. He decided to begin studying past stock guides and charts looking for patterns and price action and actual performance. He vigorously studied these chart guides, which represented past stock patterns. This dedication to study would prove to pay great rewards for him in future years. He went on to combine both fundamental and technical analysis, which he called his Techno-Fundamentalist approach, and this became the building block of his Box Theory (both described later in this chapter).

Darvas came to realize through this detailed study that there were no good or bad stocks. There were only stocks that rose in price and stocks that declined in price, and that price is based on the laws of supply and demand in the marketplace. This discovery finally taught him to trade less as he became more patient in waiting for opportunities to present themselves.

Once when he had to leave town for a month for his dancing arrangements he told his broker to handle $10,000 for him. Upon his return, Darvas discovered that his broker traded as many as 40 times during the month that he was gone. He ended up netting a profit of only $300 for the whole month. But what Darvas discovered was that his broker would sell many stocks that were rising in order to realize a small profit, and he kept the ones that continued to fall in hopes of recovering his capital. This observation led Darvas to believe that you should never sell a rising stock but always quickly sell a losing stock. He also discovered that buying higher-priced stocks was more profitable, and there was more action in those stocks. He learned from this experience and decided not to listen to the brokerage community. Darvas concluded that business is one thing and the performance of the stock of that company is another thing.

As he kept learning he realized many losses in his trades. He regarded these losses and his setbacks as his tuition on Wall Street, but he was determined to succeed. He viewed this experience as if he were trying to gain his master's degree on Wall Street. Eventually he discovered that his losses occurred due to his abandoning his rules, overconfidence when he was successful, and dispair when he was unsuccessful.

After all his study, Darvas was finally feeling like he was learning more and more and was close to putting a strategy together that would produce the results he desired. He summed up some of his discoveries and experiences. He fell for all the common temptations that nearly everyone who ventures into stocks fall for, such as:

- Low-priced stocks
- Tips and rumors
- Quality stocks that had fallen hard during a temporary drop in the overall market

He also found it was foolish to buy based solely on price alone, especially the high-priced stocks. Also, the former leaders can take a long time to come back after a correction, and most might never come back to their former levels. He discovered timing was the important thing, and it had to do with the overall behavior of the stock in the general market. It is the anticipation of growth rather than the growth itself that leads to great profits in growth stocks, he concluded. He thought it was more profitable to buy when the price was going up, and he was not interested unless it was increasing. This became his main reason for trading in stocks. He thought the market behaves the way it does due to the participants behaving the way they do, and no one knows what they will do until they actually do it.

He then summed up the long road he had taken to this point. It was actually no different than the experiences of most traders: the difference with Darvas was that he refused to give up and he stayed focused and determined to succeed. His trading system followed this typical path:

1. Tips and rumors.

2. Subscriptions to market newsletters.

3. Broker advice.

4. Stock market books (this is actually valuable, as it taught him the vocabulary of Wall Street).

5. Annual reports and fundamentals.

6. OTC stocks (small stocks with limited following).

7. Insider trading.

8. Research (industry groups, P/E ratios, stock ratings, etc.). This one caused him a $9000 loss on Jones & Laughlin.

9. Technical (price action). This is the one that proved most successful.

As he continued to develop his strategies and rules, his efforts finally began to pay off. Darvas actively traded from 1952 to the early 1960s. He made $2,450,000 from his start in the markets with the Brilund profit. He made the bulk of it in 18 months—a total of $2,250,000—after he made all the mistakes and then refined his strategy. He was so successful and talked about that the American Stock Exchange actually suspended the use of the stop-loss order (explained in detail later in this chapter) that he employed.

Once the strategies that Darvas implemented to gain his riches became public, many people started to follow his methods and utilized the stop-loss orders. There were so many stop-loss orders being placed that when they were all triggered, it caused a chain reaction of sell orders. This activity caused erratic and rapid declines in stock prices on the small American Stock Exchange and induced the exchange to suspend their use.

In May 1959, six-and a-half years after his start in the stock market and well over $2 million later in profits, he was featured in the business pages of *Time* magazine. This article caused quite a stir among Wall Streeters, as it detailed how Darvas disregarded many of the common investment practices on the street such as focusing strictly on low P/E ratio stocks, taking advice from brokers, etc. It also caused quite a bit of interest and excitement in the market, due to the success he attained, and even led to offers from publishers for Darvas to tell his entire story.

Darvas went on to write his own story in the popular book *How I Made $2,000,000 in the Stock Market.* The book sold more than 200,000 copies in just eight weeks. He then wrote a subsequent book *Wall Street: The Other Las Vegas.* The strategies he implemented to gain his riches follow.

The Darvas Method

Nicolas Darvas, through many years of trial and error, would discover, just like those before him, that there were certain skills, disciplines, and trading strategies that would emerge from his experience and begin to produce the positive results he was seeking.

Careful Skills Learned over Time

Probably the number-one trait that we could apply to Darvas was perseverance. After all, he had another profession that he was very successful with. He was not even in the securities business, but his first taste of success led him on a relentless journey that took years of hard work and study and included many frustrations. Most people would have given up long before Darvas would even attempt to continue on with the next step in the learning process. Determination and constant self-evaluation of mistakes are key traits of the very best traders. Darvas mentions in the *Time* article that he would spend nearly eight hours a day studying the market and price movements of certain stocks. This was in addition to the grueling schedule of his dance profession.

Darvas believed investors lose on their trades because of ignorance and believing in magical solutions to their problems instead of rational ones. He thought they relied too much on feeling and so-called intuition when they should be thinking instead. This led him to believe that other keys for success critical to great results were:

- Objectives
- Psychology
- The conditions in which you operate

He set his goals high, as he believed that the best speculators searched for only the very best opportunities. This correlates to what Gerald Loeb also believed, which was that the very best speculators wanted to make a killing in the market. This drive for the highest level possible is another trait of successful people in other fields as well.

Darvas also did not believe in paper trading, as that did not entail the emotional side of trading, which was one of the most difficult parts to master. He believed one simply needed to have real money on the table to test one's mental abilities. Successful traders need to understand what they are buying and what it is they hope to sell later. He viewed speculation as the basis of the buyers' estimates of how much money they might subsequently be able to sell the stock for at a future time.

Though he used charts to see and study trends, Darvas considered himself to be more of a mental chartist. He was definitely not a tape reader like Livermore or Loeb, as his professional dance engagements actually removed him far from Wall Street and the tape. He was actually more of a price movement analyst, and many times he would study the movements in the past, such as the past week, due to the retrieval of late information because of his travel schedule.

His other key secrets were self-discipline and patience. He knew to be truly successful one had to wait for the right opportunities to present themselves, and this could sometimes mean doing nothing for long periods of time. This inactivity is especially difficult for active stock traders, but the very best ones know how to control this and avoid the impulse trades and the overtrading that can be very costly to their portfolio.

The Box Theory Pays Millions

Patience paid off in the long run because Darvas knew he needed to know how to spot the rising stocks and the trends of these rising stocks. After a long, extensive study, he made a connection between what a stock might do based on what it was actually doing at the current time. He found a consistency of action and discovered the movement of stocks in trends. In both directions there were pauses or minor corrections and certain resistance levels. He viewed these changes in price like a rubber ball bouncing inside a glass box. There was a certain orderly movement and progression, but it was different for each stock.

This became the basis of his Box Theory. The progression from one box to another between clearly defined limits and then a breakthrough to a new level, which would establish another box, was positive price action in motion. This was a learned skill that he put together after many long days and nights of intense study and looking for formations and patterns. This observation skill only comes from trial and error and constant study and testing of what you actually see and what actually works in practice.

Darvas, like Loeb, also discovered that certain stocks would move with the same characteristics that could distinguish people. For example, some stocks were very volatile and some were more quiet and reserved in their performance. After years of observation and following the market as closely as these great traders did, one could get to know the movements of certain stocks and relate them to certain personality traits.

Darvas also viewed long-term investors as the real gamblers in the market due to their eternal hope of the lucky card. They would hold on to losing stocks and continuously hope for them to come back in price. As all great traders know, this is a tragic mistake and one that can cost you your entire capital, not to mention the loss of confidence that is crucial to a successful stock operator. As Darvas discovered, most of his stocks, after his rules forced him out of them, would continue to fall in price. His system preserved his capital for the next opportunity. This also protected and kept intact his confidence and actually boosted it. This confidence in his system would help him to gain control of his emotional side.

Control and Minimize Risk

Darvas learned over the years that to be a successful stock trader one had to be disciplined in his or her approach. His main consideration was to lose as little as possible when he was wrong. This strengthened his dedication to his loss-cutting strategy, which again is probably the most crucial discipline and trading rule of the five traders featured in this book. It is such an important point that it has and will be repeated many times throughout this book. Darvas wanted to control and minimize his risk. The only way to accomplish this was to discipline himself to minimize his losses on the trades that moved against him.

He would also ignore tax considerations in his sell decisions and concentrate first on making a profit in the stock. He would then let the action of the stock determine when to sell it, as opposed to ignoring the price movements of the stock and focusing on reducing taxes and the consequences of a tax law.

The Darvas Method was based on buying stocks and not on shorting stocks. Here he agreed with Loeb's thinking that it seemed harder to be as profitable on the short side of the market as opposed to the long side. Darvas found that trading in only rising or bull markets was the best chance for profits, as he also thought that because the general trend of the market over time was an upward trend, he would stay with the longer-term odds to try to reduce his risk.

As he developed the Darvas Method, which consisted of his Techno-Fundamentalist approach and the Box Theory, he also knew and realized he would:

- Be right only about half the time
- Needed a system to reduce his risks
- Have to put his pride and ego in check
- Become impartial to any stock or specific theory

He also knew that he had to change the way he thought about stocks. He had to adopt a cold, unemotional attitude toward all stocks, even the ones that provided the best performance for him. He knew he had to bring his emotions under complete control. This required an incredible amount of self-discipline in order to combat the emotions of fear, greed, hope, and ignorance that play such a large role in the market and on the individual on a daily basis.

To train his emotions, he would write down the reasons why he bought and sold each stock. If he suffered a loss on a trade, he would write down what he thought the reason was that contributed to the loss. By writing these reasons down and studying them, he would be better equipped in the future to avoid the same mistakes. He would call this his cause-of-errors table. It was a very valuable tool for him, and as we have seen from those before him and those to come, the trait of owning up to your losses using a handwritten process of review and analysis is a key trait of all these great traders. You simply must be able to face the times when you were not correct, be able to look at those losing transactions objectively, and learn from them to avoid making the same mistakes in the future. If you can repeatedly do this over and over for many years, you should learn in increments what past errors were made. By avoiding them in the future, successful traders can save quite a bit of money by not engaging in those types of transactions or cutting losses even shorter and shorter over time.

Darvas learned early on that one of the quickest ways to lose money in the market was to listen to others and all of their so-called expert opinions. He always played a lone hand after he learned that lesson and only took action based on his own study and observation. For his source of information he only relied on *Barron's*, which would come out weekly and list the actual price movements that occurred in the market. When he was traveling the world with his dance partner, he did not have the convenience of watching the tape all day. He had to rely on cablegrams being faxed to the various hotels he would stay at during his travels. These cables would quote him the prices of the stocks he was interested in. Once, when he signed a two-year dance contract around the world, the only source of information he had was his cablegrams and a week-old edition of *Barron's*. He would study the stock price movements in *Barron's* and use this source as his only base to make his trading decisions. The discipline to use only a source of facts and not open your ears to others' opinions was a key to his observations that led him to his best profits.

As he got better in his trading, he would hold only 5 to 8 stocks at one time. This was in stark contrast to his earlier days, when he was overtrading and would hold up to 30 stocks at a time. This concentration and not diversification allowed him to keep his focus on a limited number of stocks to really understand them and their price movement performance.

Darvas also discovered that there was a relationship confined within certain principles, but he thought it could not be measured exactly. What he meant by this was that he used this relationship to help him determine the general trend of the market. He discovered that it was crucial to know if the market was either in a strong bull or bear market environment. He believed and realized that most and almost all stocks would follow or be influenced by the general trend of the market. Again, the discipline to be able to trade only in the right market environment attributed to many of his successful trades.

Once the system started to work, his rules would almost automatically dictate what actions he was to take, such as buying more of an advancing issue, cutting short a loss, or staying out of the market. He discovered that his system would discipline him to ignore the emotional side of trading, and if he could constantly stick to the rules of his system, he would succeed.

Once when he had made his first half-a-million dollars in profit, he started to become overconfident and made some huge mistakes. One mistake he made was he moved closer to Wall Street (one-half mile from the Exchange) to be closer to the action. This actually caused him large losses as he lost his focus, became distracted, and began to ignore his rules. He got away from being the lone wolf and would become distracted to the point of listening to others' opinions. He lost approximately $100,000 in a few weeks as he began to overtrade and trade in desperation. His emotions were then completely out of control. Fortunately, he noticed this and decided to go back to Paris (where he would spend a lot of time performing) and back to his cable system to get back on track. After seeing his errors, he returned with his system back in place and to the disciplines that had helped him reach his first milestone.

He also knew that no one could completely master the stock market. In 1961, after his successes of millions and his bestselling book,

Darvas was still learning and tweaking his system. It proves that you always need to be a student of the market. For example, from May 1961 to January 1962, he kept taking small losses and finally quit trading during that time, as the market offered no new buys. As expected, the market slumped starting in May 1962, and Darvas was completely out of the market in order to avoid the losses that would have eventually cost him, had he ignored the general trend of the market and all the key signals his system had informed him about.

Mistakes and New Rules

Darvas created his trading rules as he kept learning from his mistakes and from his observations of what was working and what was not working in the market. It was through this process that he created The Darvas Method.

The Darvas Method consisted of what he called his Techno-Fundamentalist approach and his Box Theory. This is how he created his theories. He would not concentrate on the fallen leaders due to the heavy overhead resistance that would exist from previous buyers of the stock who had not cut short their losses. As described also by Loeb, these previous buyers would hope and wait for the fallen stock to get back to their original buy point so they could sell and get out of the transaction at a break-even point. Darvas knew this overhead resistance would hold back former leaders and keep them from making new highs. Instead, he focused on the new leaders that would be emerging with a new market cycle. He liked when these stocks would hit all-time high prices. These stocks would not have the overhead resistance to deal with, relieving the stock of a certain price level in order for it to gain new ground.

He noticed through his studies of stock price movements that stocks would trade within certain ranges. He discovered that the combination of price and increased volume was a powerful source of demand to move a stock forward. He also was not too concerned about the underlying reasons why certain stocks would just increase in price. He decided that the main reasons would actually come out after the action in the stock had occurred. As he continued his study of hundreds of charts and stock guides, he discovered that stocks did behave in certain trends and had common characteristics. They seemed to follow certain patterns over time. He noticed certain defined upward and downward trends in their chart patterns. It was within these patterns that the detail of the movement was the key. This is difficult to see, and it takes study and attention to detail to grasp. He saw within the trends that stocks would move in a series of frames that he would call boxes. The stocks would oscillate between high and low points within the framework of each box.

With the Box Theory, if a stock he was watching would create boxes that stood like a pyramid on top of each other, and would be in the highest current box, he would continue to watch the stock. The stock should bounce around within the box between the high and low, for example between $35 and $40. This would create what he would call a 35/40 box.

He would correlate this price action like the actions of a dancer. For example, a dancer would set himself in a crouch position and bounce up and down in a small manner before he would be ready to leap into the air. He viewed stocks as acting in a similar manner as they bounced around within the box frames. As long they did not violate the lower end of the box, he considered the action positive. If the stock would fall below $35 (example above), he would eliminate it from his watch list. This meant that the stock was probably not as strong as he thought it should be, and he was only interested in the stocks that were going to be the strong price leaders.

The key to this theory was to watch the stock move within the box. If it exceeded the top end of the box at $40 (example above), especially on an increase in volume, he would buy it. This would prove to him that the stock was now ready to move to the next level of boxes and had sufficient demand for an advance in price. He did not have a specific fixed rule on how this action was to take place. He would mostly do this through observation and then react quickly when it did happen.

This happens when you become familiar with the market action and the stocks you are watching day to day and then the constant observation skill you give to the task. Again, this was not easy, but the rewards paid off for him. The range of the boxes would vary between the different stocks he was watching. His challenge was to define the boxes for each stock to make sure the movement would confine a proper box for each different stock. Again, attention to detail and study were key to putting this strategy together. After trial and error with this new method, he would get better at establishing the different boxes and ranges for the stocks he was watching. In order to make sure he would catch the proper buy point of the stock at the proper time, he would place automatic "on stop" buy orders with his broker.

As the stocks would create new boxes, he would try to time his buys by buying at the closest fraction above the penetration point, or the highest point of the highest box that he would establish. He would set the purchase price as close as possible to this point as it drove through the top of the box or ceiling and into high ground. He also realized that this method was no sure-proof secret to the market, and he estimated that he would be right only about half of the time. Through many different stocks, he would buy and sell based on these new theories. He kept refining the approach as he went along and learned new ideas. In order to protect himself from the estimated 50 percent of the times he thought he would be wrong, he established his stop-loss order method for protecting his profits. The stop-loss order would instruct his broker to sell his positions when the stock declined to a set price that Darvas would give for each stock he was holding.

The keys to this Box Theory were looking for high volume increases as the stock moved higher, especially in the smaller issues. He would use the box to establish the price for the buy if and only if it broke through the top of the box on an increase in volume. Once this happened, he knew he had to keep hold of a rising stock and not to sell too early, and to limit his losses when he was wrong.

The Box Theory was based on the following presumptions, and he was now ready to set his new objectives.

- He would buy only the right stocks (rising stocks).
- He needed to have his timing correct (stocks hitting new highs).
- He had to contain his mistakes to small and limiting losses.
- He would let his big profits (his big winners) run until they proved otherwise.

The tools he would utilize to accomplish these new objectives were:

- Focus exclusively on price and volume action
- His Box Theory
- Use of automatic "on-stop" buy orders
- Limit his losses and control risk using stop-loss sell orders

With his new system, he decided he would just follow a strong stock's path upward, raising his stop-loss order behind him as the price of the stock kept increasing. If the trend continued upward, he would buy more stock, or pyramid up, and if it reversed he would sell out and minimize his loss.

This strategy caused him to lean more toward the technical side of the market and simple observation, but he also believed that the best fundamental stocks performed even better because the analysts would study them and advise mutual fund managers to purchase them. The activity of mutual fund managers buying these recommended stocks would add buying power to the stock and hopefully contribute to the increase in its price. This would increase the chance of these stocks becoming the new leaders. These would also be the ones with the best-expected earnings for the future. He considered this an important part of a stock's price movement. This allowed him to take a longer view than just the technical side, and he combined the two for a complete analysis of stocks.

He now would look at the following concerning fundamentals:

- The capitalization of the company
- The industry group that the stock belonged to
- The expected earnings of the company for upcoming quarters

He would use the following when evaluating technical action:

- The Box Theory
- The volume of the stock as it traded
- The historical peak price of the stock

This is what he now called his Techno-Fundamentalist approach. This approach, combined with his Box Theory, was the formation of the strategy that would lead to his success in the market.

Along the way Darvas found that the minor fluctuations in the market were a distraction and involved too much guesswork. He discovered that when he was away and not looking for each minor change in the market that he did much better. This was a different approach from Livermore and Loeb, who were constant tape readers. Because of his approach, Darvas would utilize stop-loss orders as his risk control mechanism for cutting his losses short. So it did not matter that his approach to the day-to-day monitoring of the market was different than Livermore and Loeb's tape-reading approach; they all recognized the important need for a strict loss-cutting rule.

In August 1957, nearly five years after his experience with Brilund, market action forced Darvas out of every single stock he owned. He found there was nothing attractive to buy. Sure enough, a baby bear market then hit stocks. He found that it was hard to determine when a turning point appeared, but it was easy to see after the fact. He relied totally on his stocks that were following his rules to determine when those turning points were occurring.

During this baby bear market in 1957, he began studying further and stayed out of the market. He discovered that the former leaders would not likely be the leaders of the next up market. He studied the stocks that would decline the least during this correction. He thought that they would have the best opportunity to be the new leaders. Most of these stocks also possessed the best fundamental characteristics as well. This was a strong reason why he developed his techno-fundamentalist approach. His theory was that earnings and the future estimate of increased earnings were the keys from a fundamental approach, and would be the key drivers of higher stock prices. He would then try to look out 20 years for future industries and demand for products and try to target those companies that would try to meet that demand. Though this outlook was very difficult because of the time frame involved, he would try to see what demands in the future could have the most impact on certain stocks and industries.

In the fall of 1957, the system that Darvas had painstakingly been putting together started to work with a stock called Lorillard. He purchased this stock after watching it rise from $17 to $27 on increased volume. He stayed patient with this stock, and he set up a box of 24/27 and started to buy as it kept rising through the tops of his established boxes. The 24/27 box meant that he thought the stock would trade between the range of $24 to $27, based on its recent action. If the stock dropped below $24, he would sell out his shares and move on to another opportunity. If it broke out above $27, he thought he had a real leader and its prospects for further advances would be high, especially if the increased prices came on larger than normal volume. He kept buying Lorillard as the stock increased in price, and he took advantage of margin to leverage his trade. Darvas would also use what he called pilot buys to test the direction of a stock. This was the same strategy as Livermore's probing strategy that he was using to test his stocks many decades earlier. Darvas would also use his Box Theory to implement his pyramiding strategy to continue buying a strong rising stock as it kept advancing in price.

In five months, Lorillard and Diner's Club, another stock he was purchasing using his method, produced profits of $21,000, and he doubled his capital. He used margin on both stocks to leverage his gains.

He then made a mistake by buying Lorillard back at three different times due to his prior success with the stock. He ended up taking three small losses and learned the lesson of not having to think that just because a stock provided large profits before, that he could and should be able to do it again with the same stock. You must keep looking for the next stock with the right characteristics instead of the same old familiar names that might have worked very profitably for you in the past.

His confidence in his system began to grow, and he then started watching a stock called E.L. Bruce. He started buying this stock in May 1958, and he bought the stock five different times, in lots of 500 shares each, all at higher prices as the stock kept advancing. He had a stop loss order put in at $48 per share. His purchases looked like this:

500 shares @ $50.75	$25,510.95
500 shares @ $51.125	$25,698.90
500 shares @ $51.75	$26,012.20
500 shares @ $52.75	$26,513.45
500 shares @ $53.625	<u>$26,952.05</u>
	$130,687.55

E.L. Bruce continued to rise dramatically, and by June 13th it was trading at $77 per share. Darvas now had a fast-rising star, and his patience and experience told him to hang on to a winner until it proved otherwise. Darvas was then told that the American Stock Exchange had suspended trading in E.L. Bruce due to a group who was trying to take control of the company and buy out the stock. This action was the initial cause for the stock to increase in price, but Darvas knew nothing about this at the time that his rules alerted him to the action of the stock, which is why he began purchasing it. Because there were also many short sellers in the stock, as they viewed it as overvalued while the stock kept rising, they could not cover their short positions.

This action caused a disorderly market in the stock, which is why the exchange suspended trading. Because the short sellers still had to cover their positions, they were willing to pay $100 per share in the over-the-counter market. As Darvas held fast to his stock due to the rising demand, he held on for two more weeks and then finally sold out at increments of 100 or 200 shares at an average price of $171 per share. His profit on the transactions amounted to more than $295,300.

At this time Darvas had made approximately $325,000 in nine months with his success in Lorillard and E.L. Bruce. He became more cautious, withdrawing one-quarter of his capital and put it away for safekeeping. This money management skill of taking profits and putting it away for reserve would serve him well as he continued to build his capital base.

With the first real successes tested with his new system, he would continue with his methods with two additional stocks, which were Universal Controls and Thiokol. After observation and buying at the right times with his Box Theory, he was sitting on over a half-million dollars in paper profits when he started to become overconfident.

As mentioned earlier, Darvas had moved close to Wall Street, lost his focus, became distracted, abandoned his rules, and found himself facing nearly $100,000 in losses on other bad trades. After acknowledging his mistakes and going to Paris to recollect himself, he returned to the United States to continue his trading. He devoted himself to his rules, which he felt confident in and had shown him what he was capable of if he kept his discipline and stuck to his hard-earned strategy.

He kept trading in promising stocks and cutting losses on losing stocks, and he still held strong positions in Universal Controls and Thiokol. They kept rising and he kept holding, as there were no good reasons to sell strong upward-trending stocks. All these trades were done through telegram and not speaking to his brokers. He wanted absolutely no other opinions to play into his trading strategy. After Universal rocketed from $66 to $102 in three weeks, he noticed that the rapid rise would not last and as the stock began to turn directions, Darvas noticed the weakening of the stock and sold out his positions between $86.25 and $89.75. Though this was off the high, Darvas always said no one could buy at the absolute lowest price and sell at the absolute highest price. His profit nonetheless was more than $409,350.

His next big winner was Texas Instruments, which he started buying at $94.362 and made another add-on purchase at $97.875. He then made an additional purchase at $101.875 as the stock kept rising in price. Imagine how scary these transactions must have seemed to most investors, as Darvas would make these initial buys at the highest price and then add to them at higher and higher prices.

Meanwhile his stake in Thiokol was continuing to act very well. After a three-for-one split in the stock, Darvas was finally stopped out of Thiokol, but it would turn out to be his most profitable trade. His profit on Thiokol was more than $862,000.

In the spring of 1959, with more than a million dollars in stock market profits, he made new pilot buys into four strong fundamental and technical stocks he had been watching for quite a while. Beckman Industries and Litton Industries did not work out, and he was stopped out with small losses. He then put more money into the other two, which had acted as he expected, Zenith Radio and Fairchild Camera.

He kept his system in place until he was finally stopped out of these three strong remaining stocks. When he finally sold Texas Instruments, Zenith Radio, and Fairchild Camera, his total profits during the seven years since he started with the Brilund transaction was more than $2,000,000.

The Darvas Box Theory kept him out of declining or bear markets. Because the lack of advancing stocks would not create the boxes he was looking for, he would not purchase anything. This was a key trading rule and discipline of his, which helped provide the ability to stay on the sidelines when the market offered no new good buying opportunities.

Darvas would also have a very high percentage of his capital in a single issue of stock, sometimes as much as 50 percent, if he knew he was right. For example, he had 50 percent of his capital in Texas Instruments when he made his final purchase in this stock. This is also a strategy he was more comfortable with as he grew more successful and developed more experience over time.

Applying the Box Theory to Current Times

As we showed with Livermore, we will use Darvas's trading rules and apply them to a leader in the current market environment. Omnivision Technologies (OVTI) is a leader in the Semiconductor–Electronics group that designs, develops, and markets semiconductor imaging devices for computing, communications, and electronics applications. Fundamentals of the company have been outstanding recently. The January 31, 2003 fiscal quarter showed a 999-percent increase in earnings and a 206-percent increase in revenues. The fiscal quarter ended April 2003 showed a 243-percent increase in earnings and a 204-percent increase in revenues. As mentioned before, the NASDAQ market was leading the new uptrend that started in mid-March 2003, and Omnivision was soon to follow shortly thereafter. Figure 4-1 shows the daily activity of Omnivision from April 2003 through September 2003. The stock more than doubled during this brief six-month period.

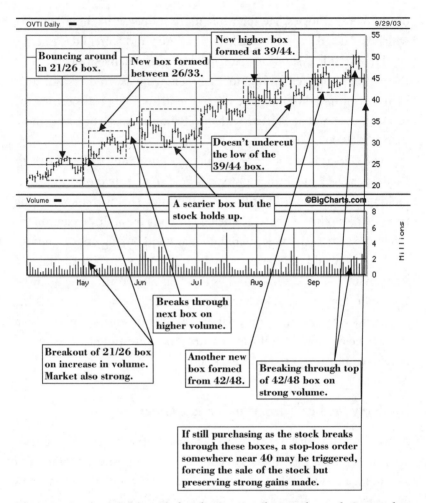

Figure 4-1   Omnivision Technologies. April 2003 through September 2003. Source: *www.bigcharts.com.*

Notice the stair-step pattern of the boxes as the stock kept climbing upward. The boxes also take into account the minor daily fluctuations that all stocks go through. However, in the best winning stocks, these types of patterns usually do not violate the trading rules formulated. If they do, the stop-loss order is there to protect the gains and minimize the downside risk.

Nicolas Darvas is an interesting example of someone who refused to quit and give in. His determination and perseverance to succeed was a major reason for the success that finally came his way after many years of study and developing his theories and methods.

5

William J. O'Neil

"...with persistence and hard work, anything is possible. You can do it, and your own determination to succeed is the most important element."

=====

The Chairman of Research

William J. O'Neil was born in 1933 in Oklahoma City and raised in Texas. He joined the Air Force, worked his way through college, and graduated from Southern Methodist University. All the while, he was interested in the stock market. He began his career as a stockbroker with Hayden, Stone & Co. in 1958 after graduation from college.

It was during his early days at Hayden, Stone & Co. that O'Neil decided he liked the research side of the business as opposed to the sales side, which is where he had been spending most of his time. O'Neil's trading career started off like many others: by subscribing to a few investment newsletters and buying low P/E ratio stocks. His results did not show much success, and he continued reading many books on the stock market. In 1959, one year after he became a stockbroker, he noticed that the Dreyfus Fund had performed much better than all the other funds. Relatively small at $15 million, the fund was managed by Jack Dreyfus. The results of the Dreyfus Fund were twice as strong as all the other funds at that time.

O'Neil was so intrigued by the success of this fund that he decided to study every stock the fund purchased over the prior two-year period. He sent away for the fund prospectus and quarterly reports that would identify which stocks the fund had purchased, and he then studied the chart patterns of these stocks. The discovery he made changed his view on how to buy stocks and became the building block that led to the development of his strategy.

Through his extensive study, O'Neil discovered that of the approximately 100 stocks the fund had purchased from 1957 to 1959, all were purchased when the stocks actually reached new highs in price after correcting and setting up in a base-building pattern. A chartist and a tape reader, Jack Dreyfus was buying every stock for his fund at a new high in price after the stocks were coming out of sound basing patterns.

This discovery led O'Neil to develop his own set of rules based on researching common characteristics of the leading stocks in terms of price performance. It took him about two or three years to put his system together. At about the same time (in 1960), he was accepted to Harvard Business School's first Program for Management Development (PMD). While at Harvard, one of the books he read was *How to Trade in Stocks* by Jesse Livermore. He learned from that book that his objective in the market should be to lose the least amount of money when he was wrong and to be sure to make the big money when he was right.

Using his own rules, formulated through his trading experiences and testing, O'Neil went on to increase his personal portfolio more than twentyfold in 18 months from late 1962 to 1964.

O'Neil made his first trade in the market with only $500, which is all he had at the time. It proves once again, as many of the traders featured in this book have demonstrated, that it's possible to start with a limited capital stake, and, through proper discipline and adherence to rules, grow it into a substantial amount over time.

The new rules he was developing became known as the CAN SLIM method, and it is discussed later in this chapter. The first stock he purchased using this method was Universal Match in February 1960. It doubled in price in 16 weeks. However, he sold the stock too quickly and didn't make much on the trade, largely because he did not have much money to invest at the time. He next bought Procter & Gamble, Reynolds' Tobacco, and MGM following the same rules. Again, these all did well, but due to his limited capital, his gains were minimal.

From Jesse Livermore's *How to Trade in Stocks*, O'Neil began adopting the strategy of pyramiding up, or buying more of a stock as it continued to rise in price. Because O'Neil's new rules seemed to be getting him into the right stocks at the right time, the pyramiding strategy would only leverage his gains. As a result, his trading profits began to improve.

During the first half of 1961, O'Neil did well in his trades with Great Western Financial, Brunswick, Kerr-McGee, Crown Cork & Seal, AMF, and Certain-teed. But by the summer of 1961, the market started to turn down, and all of his gains evaporated. He had discovered that although he had bought correctly, he held on too long as the market shifted directions. He then spent the remainder of 1961 analyzing every transaction he had made that year. This analysis is finally what put him on the right path. You might remember that we saw this kind of self-analysis as a key trait in all the other successful traders before him.

During his analysis, O'Neil noticed that when he correctly bought Certain-teed in the low 20s after a pullback from its initial base, he sold and was quickly shaken out with only a 2- or 3-point profit. This quick action (similar to what we saw with Darvas when he adopted the old strategy of "you can never go broke by taking a profit") actually would turn out to be a huge opportunity cost. In this example, Certain-teed later went on to triple in price.

O'Neil concluded that he would buy stocks as close to their pivot points as possible and not pyramid up on the stock if it had increased 5 percent or more past this point. He would buy more if the stock increased 2½ percent or 3 percent above the pivot point from his initial buy. This action indicated to him that he was probably right, and the stock was going to continue to move up in price, but he wanted to control the risk. He also decided he would sell when he had 20-percent to 25-percent gains in his stocks but he would try to hold fast-rising stocks longer if their action did not warrant sell signals. This patience concerning the time element (the best profits don't happen overnight, and the road to success is a learning process) would pay off big for him in his future years.

He discovered that successful growth stocks usually rise between 20 percent to 25 percent and then decline and begin to build new bases and then resume their advance. He also noted when stocks took off quickly past their pivot point and gained 20 percent within the first three weeks, these stocks tended to become the very best gainers and must be held for at least eight weeks, then re-appraised and probably held much longer. His new plan was to take profits at 20 percent when he had them, except for these most powerful stocks that gain that same amount in the shortest period of time, and to cut his losses quickly at 8 percent below his buy point. He also discovered the advantage of pyramiding, providing he kept his add-on purchases within 3 percent of the original purchase, as it would force him to move his money into his strongest stocks. The other discovery he made, when all his early 1961 gains evaporated, was that the action of the leading stocks topping (when they stopped advancing) would most likely signal that the general market would begin declines of 10 percent or more. This is when he began to study and concentrate on the action of the general market.

O'Neil's studies revealed how the markets' movement as a whole affected individual stocks. Three months later, his rules took him out of every stock he had, strictly due to their individual action and on the action of the general market. He was 100 percent in cash when the market started to head for a big drop in the spring of 1962 (the same rules got him 100 percent in cash before the 1987 bad market break).

After reading Edwin Lefevre's *Reminiscences of a Stock Operator*, O'Neil saw the parallel between the market of 1907 and the then current situation of 1962. He then began to sell short Certain-teed, which was actually on the recommended buy list of Hayden, Stone & Co. at the time. Shorting the stock subjected him to criticism from the firm because he was still employed there. He also shorted Korvette in late 1962, and the profits from these short transactions were substantial.

In October 1962, after the Cuban Missile Crisis subsided, the Dow increased and began turning upward after it showed a classic follow-through confirmation. O'Neil bought Chrysler at $58 per share, as it was one of the first new leaders coming off the market bottom. Throughout a strong market in 1963, he followed his rules and did exceptionally well. Many of his accounts were up several hundred percent, and he limited his losses to 5 percent and 6 percent. One of his best performers was Syntex, which he had purchased at $100 per share in June 1963 (it was up 40 percent in eight weeks). He held on and ran it out for six months.

While success might have come relatively quickly for O'Neil, it wasn't always easy. He spent many long nights studying in order to put his plan and strategy together. It also took some in-depth analysis of his mistakes, the drive to correct those mistakes, and the discipline not to repeat them.

His great success during the 1962 and 1963 periods were accomplished with three exceptional trades back-to-back-to-back increasing his $5000 stake at the time to $200,000, using some borrowed funds and margin to leverage his account. Those trades were, short Korvette, long Chrysler, and long Syntex. This financial success allowed O'Neil to be one of the youngest ever (at age 30) to purchase a seat on The New York Stock Exchange. It was at this point that he struck out on his own, leaving Hayden, Stone. It was also during this time that he really started to do extensive stock research and began creating the first U.S. stock daily database.

Cutting-Edge Research

In California, O'Neil started his own company called William O'Neil & Co., which was to become a securities research firm servicing institutional investment firms. His firm created the first and most comprehensive stock market database in the industry. It is currently one of the most respected securities research firms in the country, serving more than 600 major institutional accounts and tracking over 3000 technical and fundamental data items on over 10,000 different publicly traded stocks. His company also covers data on over 9600 mutual funds. One of the first products offered by William O'Neil & Company was the O'Neil database datagraph books. Today, each book displays 98 different fundamental and 27 different technical items for each stock. These books still exist today but have mostly been replaced by WONDA (William O'Neil Direct Access). This service is a direct Web access link to the O'Neil database. WONDA was originally created for O'Neil's in-house money managers but is now available for institutional clients. He also owns Daily Graphs, Inc., a company that produces printed chart books and offers a Web-based chart service for individual investors.

Through his extensive continuing study of what caused certain stocks to increase in price more than others, O'Neil discovered that the very best stocks shared certain common characteristics before they began their impressive price moves. The study that he performed went back to 1953, and he has put the findings into a resource that is called "The Model Book of Greatest Stock Market Winners," which features more than 600 of the greatest performing stocks over the past 50 years. He uses this historical research as the basis for his investment strategy.

William J. O'Neil is probably best known to the general public as the Founder and Chairman of *Investor's Business Daily (IBD)*. *IBD* is an innovative fast growing business newspaper publication, nearly every year increasing its reader base and taking away market share from *The Wall Street Journal.* O'Neil founded *IBD* in April 1984 with a base of only 15,000 subscribers, as he sought to develop a better way to provide more useful investment information to the public. Today, the estimated daily readership of *IBD* is more than 800,000. The national newspaper, which for many years did not make a profit, was financed strictly on profits made from his own stock trades. It was thought *IBD* would be for CEOs. It has turned out to be a much more useful product for individual investors at all levels. Due to *IBD's* many proprietary ratings and tables, the individual investor has an independent, reliable tool to access and research market information in an unbiased view. It is based on factual research going back to his study of successful stock models. New ideas for *IBD* are usually beta tested for up to one year before they are introduced to the public in the paper. *IBD* is really a computer printout and evaluation tool of the entire market. It also acts as a screening tool with extensive research, analysis, and proprietary ratings.

Using the investment rules he formulated over the years and the research he conducted that was instrumental in creating *IBD*, O'Neil has attained some of the best published returns in stock trading. He bought Pic'N Save in late 1976 and held it for 7 ½ years for a twentyfold increase. He bought Price Company and realized a tenfold increase in 3½ years coming off the bottom of the 1982 bear market. Coming off the bottom of the October 1998 market, he purchased America OnLine (AOL) and Charles Schwab & Co. and made 456 percent and

313 percent, respectively, from the pivot buy point to when he sold out his positions on the way up.

In 1990 and 1991, he bought Amgen on numerous days and spread out his buys. Add-on purchases were made when there were significant gains on previous buys. If the current price was 20 points over his average cost and a new pivot point occurred off a proper base, he would buy more. This is a sophisticated pyramiding strategy that should only be attempted by very experienced investors.

O'Neil's personal stock investment account averaged more than 40 percent annually during the 1980s. He realized gains of 401 percent in 1998 and 322 percent in 1999. His biggest winners during that period were AOL, Charles Schwab, Qualcomm, and Sun Microsystems (charts shown at the end of this chapter). It was his second best performance period ever, followed only by his initial success in the early 1960s.

He was also noted for placing a full-page advertisement in *The Wall Street Journal* in early 1982, stating stocks had reached their lows, and that people should invest in defense-electronics and certain consumer growth stocks. In that year, internal money managers at his firm started purchasing stocks on full margin and had their best performance ever up to that point. From 1978 to 1991, their account was up twentyfold. Beginning in 1998 to 2000, their account was up 1500 percent.

The method O'Neil devised for his trading rules is called the CAN SLIM investment research tool. Each letter of the CAN SLIM acronym stands for a certain characteristic that is common to all the greatest stocks going back to 1953. How well has this method worked? David Ryan and Lee Freestone (independent individual investors), among others who used CAN SLIM in the 1980s and 1990s, both have won national investing championships with real money. There are also tens of thousands of other confirmed success stories of dedicated *IBD* readers who have followed the CAN SLIM method for a number of years and have realized and kept substantial profits, especially during the great bull market years of the late 1990s.

O'Neil published his first book in 1988 titled *How to Make Money in Stocks*. It was the bestselling investment book of that year, and has since sold well over one million copies. Its third edition published in 2002. In 2000, he published *24 Essentials Lessons for Investment Success,* which also became a top seller. In 2003, he published his third book, *The Successful Investor*. I highly encourage you to read all of these publications at least a few times, as they illustrate the correct strategies of the CAN SLIM method in great detail. O'Neil also provides Advanced Investment Workshops, usually to sold-out audiences, a few times a year in select major cities that offer the chance for the individual investor to see and hear his strategies in person.

The CAN SLIM Strategy

Vital Skills Are First Required

One trait that has been used to describe William O'Neil in various interviews is his relentless energy and hard work ethic. As the great traders before him all possessed, we have seen that the amount of time devoted to the study of the details and the market was a key trait and required skill of all. There is simply no substitute for hard work if you want to succeed, especially if you want to be one of the best. In the stock market, as we've mentioned before, it is no different. O'Neil is a steadfast believer in the effort that must be put forth to produce profitable results in the ever-challenging environment of the stock market.

O'Neil believes it takes time, study, diligence, and persistence to fully understand and participate within the boundaries of the market for success. His early days included many long nights of chart study before he felt he understood how the market actually works. It was through the discoveries during these studies that he began to build his rules on fact-based knowledge. His rules are also based on reducing risk to the lowest possible point while trying to increase the returns to the greatest possibilities. This high-level goal is something we saw in previous traders as well. It's the drive to achieve at the highest level and having ambitious goals that ultimately lead to the realization of those goals. Many investors have materially benefited from using his CAN SLIM system.

O'Neil's system uses both fundamental and technical analysis in his trading rules. His choice is to not be closed-minded to only one type of analysis, which is what many investors do, but instead is based on looking at the facts of what and how the market actually works. If the market, based on exhaustive study, proves that the greatest performing stocks over the last 50 years showed common characteristics of both fundamentals and technical price action, then why argue with how the market actually works?

Remember what Jesse Livermore said in the twentieth century: "The stock market never really changes that much. What happened before will happen again and again and again…" This saying has been proven again by O'Neil's detailed research of recurring stock patterns. This is truly a skill all future great traders need to have: the ability to look at objective facts and history instead of relying on someone else's personal opinion or tips and touts.

O'Neil also believes that it's good to get kicked around in the market and lose some money. He too viewed these losses as the required tuition you pay on Wall Street, noting that traders can refine their skills once they learn from their mistakes. Losses also test one's emotions and show how important it is to establish sound trading rules in order to control the emotional side of stock investing.

He views the best investors as decisive individuals without huge egos. To be successful in the market rarely has to do with intelligence. Humility and common sense provide the necessary balance. O'Neil mentions many times in his books that he personally has known more than a few individuals who, despite their occupational success and intelligence, suffered severe losses in the market. They either thought they were smarter than the market, did not follow sound trading rules, or a combination of the two. The stock market is simply a dangerous place for egos or dishonesty. To succeed in the market you must leave your ego behind when the bell rings.

O'Neil believes in keeping the process simple and basic. There are just too many technical indicators out there that don't have as detailed a track record of success as pure volume and price action based on good, fundamentally sound stocks. And to prove this method works, each of the greats featured in this book looked at volume and price action as the most important aspects for stock trading.

O'Neil also believed in concentration and focus. Instead of trying to follow many different indicators that are out there, he concentrates on only the time-proven ones that produce the measure of demand in the market. These are the trends of the general market and leading stocks and how they perform based on daily volume and price action.

Luck plays no part in gaining long-term success trading stocks. It takes hard work, persistence, and trial and error to refine your skills. O'Neil has found that only 1 or 2 out of every 10 stocks you buy will truly turn out to be outstanding and capable of large gains. You need to cut your losses short so your thinking does not become unfocused, and you must make sure you can think rationally. With experience, both your results and your skill level will improve if you stick to your rules.

Discipline and Facts

O'Neil could be described as both a positive thinker and a strict disciplinarian. He has kept to the facts and the reality of what actually worked in the market over a long period of time, and his discipline has contributed handsomely to his success.

He is mostly bullish and very optimistic about the opportunities in American companies due to the vast entrepreneurial spirit and track record of success in this great country. Because history has produced an overall upward trend in the market over the years, he is much disciplined in his approach of staying fully invested in bull markets and mostly on the sidelines during bear markets. In 1989, he stated that he only made significant profits in two of the prior nine bear markets, and he estimates that he has been profitable on approximately 66 percent of his trades.

As mentioned previously, and just as the other greats before him also did, O'Neil performs a postanalysis of all his trades. At the end of each year he reviews and marks on each chart the exact price he purchased the stock for and then the exact price he sold the stock for. Then, and perhaps most important, he states the reasons why he made each purchase and sale. He uses these notes to keep learning from both the mistakes he made and what reasons produced the winners. He also believes that when you buy a stock, you should write down the potential price you'll sell the stock for before you actually sell it.

From his loss-cutting rule, it is either 7 percent or 8 percent below the purchase price. In his best growth stocks, he targets a top selling price of 130 percent growth in the P/E ratio from when he bought it. In more challenging markets, he looks for 20-percent gains. Here he uses the P/E ratio expansion as a measure of when to sell after a large increase as opposed to a buy measure based on how low the PE might seem (similar to how Loeb utilized the P/E ratio). This discipline to the handwritten policy proves for him that the hard analysis of your past decisions is a key learning tool to keep you from getting into trouble in the market and deviating from sound buy and sell rules.

The fundamentals of a stock play a large factor in his decision to purchase, as he believes it is crucial to get to know what the company does. Another characteristic of a potential target is that the best performers usually introduce some new product or service offerings. The best stocks represent companies that simply pave new avenues for businesses or consumers, which leads to a strong and increased demand for their products and/or services, causing increased profit streams to those companies. This fact has proven itself over and over again, as each new market cycle produces new names with new ideas and offerings.

Once O'Neil has studied the fundamentals searching for the very best stocks to buy, he uses technical clues to guide him on when to actually purchase the stock and to alert him to problems well before the fundamentals will indicate to sell the stock. He has proven that correct chart analysis is very important, and if done correctly, assists in timing for profitable results.

Again, this has been proven over the years, especially during the most recent bear market that began in 2000. Many high-ranking, strong, fundamental stocks started to break down well before the financials supported the weakness of the stock or negative news was made public. Enron and WorldCom were the most extreme recent examples of late. This is because the market always discounts news and looks ahead (usually up to six months). You simply should not trade on news; you should trade on what the market is currently doing at the time. This takes extreme discipline, especially in today's environment, as it seems confusing market news and opinion are more common and prevalent from many different sources.

Of all the technical and market indicators available to traders today, you must be able to discipline yourself to filter out the less important ones. Psychological indicators should only be used as secondary indicators after the general market and the price action of the leading stocks. Some of the more valuable secondary indicators include the put/call ratio, and the bulls and bears investment advisory statistics, which state how many investment newsletter writers are either bullish or bearish. But there simply is no need to concern yourself with all of the less reliable indicators. The action of the market itself and the leading stocks will dictate to you what needs to be done.

Regarding taxes, O'Neil also believed them to be a secondary consideration when looking at a trade, as did the great traders Loeb and Darvas. First, you must work to get the highest return possible using sound rules and disciplines and not changing these rules based on tax issues. Your initial goal is to make a profit, and a large one at that, and then you should look at tax consequences as a secondary concern.

Consistent with all the other great traders featured is O'Neil's belief in not overdiversifying. Instead, he would keep his concentration on the very best stocks and watch them carefully. He believes in even allocation. For example, if you have $100,000 to invest, you only need to invest in five or six stocks. You should not buy all the stocks at the same time, but allocate an approximate even amount for each issue. This concentration and focus is what leads to the best returns. Then you can weed out the weakest ones and follow up and allocate more to the strongest performers. This is similar in strategy to how Loeb would prune his portfolio at certain times, eliminating the worst 10 percent of his performers. This discipline allows you to focus better and follow the daily price movements of your stocks looking for clues to buy more, sell some or all, or hold your positions.

O'Neil believes in disciplining yourself to evaluate the market closely every day, as turns in general market direction can come fast and without warning. He notes that bear markets usually end when business is still in a downtrend, and in bull markets business conditions usually start to slow or decline before a recession sets in—and especially before a recession is officially announced. These are the forward-looking elements of the market and you need to be disciplined in your daily study to notice them.

Understanding how markets act during different cycles is also crucial. Bear markets usually open strong and close weak, and in bull markets, days usually open weak and close strong. Growth stocks usually peak when their earnings are still solid and most analyst estimates are rosy. It takes a keen eye and the ability to filter out the noise to objectively concentrate on strictly what the market is doing and not to get distracted from the facts.

O'Neil does not believe in using stop orders, but he prefers market orders. He thinks that stop-loss orders show your hand to the market makers, which can allow the market makers to try to force your order to be executed by dropping the stock. However, these stop-loss orders can provide some benefit if you can't watch the market every day (such was the case with Darvas). This then becomes your protection against adverse moves. Stop-losses also can discipline your sell side if you find yourself unable to stick to an automatic market order loss-cutting strategy.

In disciplining yourself to study the market each day, it is crucial to understand historical patterns. When markets top and stop increasing in their advance, they will usually always show you no more new proper buy candidates, as the leaders are beginning to top out and no new good bases are forming. As for spotting market bottoms, sessions when the averages close higher than the day before is the beginning of an attempted rally.

However, you then need the follow-through day to tell you if the rally has been confirmed or not. The follow-through day should have the major averages rising 1.7 percent to 2 percent or greater with a noticeable increase in volume. The best occur between the 4th and the 7th days. Some confirmations can occur from the 10th to the 20th day. The follow-through day gives you the confidence to begin looking for attractive buys of leading stocks that are breaking out of sound bases. No new bull market has ever begun without a follow-through confirmation, though it does not mean all will succeed. The best opportunities usually occur within the first two years of a new bull market, so it pays to be ever observant.

O'Neil is a big believer in doing your own research and making your own investment decisions. His whole strategy and the publication of *IBD* are based on this premise. Few analyst recommendations are correct. Instead of relying heavily on analysts' personal opinions and recommendations, one should use only historical facts, conduct their own research, study, and come to their own conclusions.

While Livermore and Loeb were professional tape readers (along with Jack Dreyfus), O'Neil believes tape reading is difficult and can become emotional (due to the higher chances of getting "caught up" in the action of a stock that you are continuously watching). To do it properly, it involves viewing the tape objectively and getting a feel for the market and its current action and direction, and that takes experience. Observant tape readers like Livermore and Loeb could tell whom the new leaders were going to be coming off declines. O'Neil's publications alert serious individual investors to these opportunities without having to view the tape constantly throughout the day.

Never-Fail Rules

I highly recommended that you read O'Neil's publications *How to Make Money in Stocks, 24 Essential Lessons for Investment Success,* and *The Successful Investor* to fully understand the details of his strategies. You can also visit his *investors.com* Web site, which has a learning center. This chapter is intended only to summarize the major points of his detailed methods.

Before we begin to discuss the CAN SLIM investment research tool, we need to address O'Neil's number-one trading rule: his loss-cutting strategy. He advocates cutting all losses at 7 percent to 8 percent below the purchase price you paid for the stock. This is his insurance policy to protect against much larger potential losses. He sets it at that rate due to the fact that by using charts correctly and timing the market, you should be able to keep your losses at those manageable levels. Over time, experience will allow you to cut them even shorter. He believes that how an investor thinks about losses is crucial, as most people lose money in the market because they simply cannot accept taking small losses and admitting they were wrong in their initial buy decisions. This rule serves as the basis for eliminating one of the most difficult things to do in stock trading, which is to remove the emotional part of selling and trading. Following this loss-cutting rule forces you to adhere to a strict set rule, and the process then becomes automatic. Emotions in investor psychology are so strong that you must develop strict rules and follow them diligently.

As O'Neil states, all stocks are bad and there are no good stocks unless they go up in price. This is similar in thought to the other great traders profiled in this book. Here again we see the most important rule is the loss-cutting rule to protect your capital. Probably nowhere has this proven more true than the bear market that began in March 2000. Those who didn't follow this cardinal O'Neil and *IBD* rule have probably suffered devastating losses over the past few years.

As mentioned earlier, historical research of how the market has actually worked for nearly half a century helped O'Neil build models of what characteristics the best performing stocks had just prior to making their incredible moves upward in price. This study also kept him from listening to others and all of the so-called experts. His rules are based solely on how the market actually works, and he listens only to these time-tested and successful rules instead of getting polluted by outside influences and naysayers.

The CAN SLIM method is made up of approximately 60 percent analysis devoted to fundamentals and 40 percent to technical analysis. O'Neil conducts extensive research into the fundamentals to find the very best stocks to invest in, and he uses technical analysis to time the optimum buy and sell points of individual stocks.

O'Neil's trading strategy is based on extensive research of the greatest performing stocks since 1953. Each letter in the CAN SLIM acronym stands for a key characteristic of the greatest performing stocks before their greatest price advances. A summary of each of the seven characteristics follows.

C—Current Quarterly Earnings per Share

This fundamental trait stood out as the most important with the biggest winners. This method stresses choosing only the very best stocks. Due to the heavy emphasis on profitable performance of a company to drive stock prices, O'Neil looks for quarterly earnings to be growing at rates of 25 percent or more. Of the 600 best performing stocks since 1953, 75 percent of them had earnings increases of greater than 70 percent in the quarter prior to the beginning of their large price advances. The other 25 percent had a 90-percent increase the very next quarter. Sales, also a fundamental trait, shows strong demand for a company's product or services and these great stocks had increases of more than 25 percent. Acceleration of sales and earnings growth rates is also very important, and the stronger the acceleration the better.

His studies have proven that profitability is one of the main keys to the performance of a stock, just like many of his predecessors believed. He has discovered that three out of four of the biggest winners were growth stocks that showed 30 percent or greater increases in EPS (earnings per share) growth rates for the prior three-year period before they made their big moves. Growth stocks are defined as those companies that average at least 20 percent growth in sales and earnings on an annual basis. They will usually have higher P/E ratios than most other stocks, and the best usually have ROE's (return on equity ratios) of greater than 17 percent. The best performing stocks of the 1990s had P/E ratios of 31 before their large price moves. These P/E ratios then went on to the 70s range during their price rise.

Investors who adhere strictly to low P/E ratio stocks would simply have missed out on the very best winners, due to their having what value investors would consider too high a ratio at the opportune time to buy these stocks. Earnings and sales growth are simply the main keys in the fundamentals that have contributed to the best gains over time. This is just a fact, and it has been seen over and over and cycle after cycle in the stock market. The strong earnings and expectation of great future earnings is one of the main reasons why professionals bid up prices of certain stocks.

A—ANNUAL EARNINGS INCREASES

Look for annual earnings increases of a minimum of 25 percent for each of the last three years. EPS ratings in *IBD* combine the two most recent quarters' earnings growth rates and the three-year annual growth rate. They are then compared to all other public companies.

You want to seek ratings of 80 (out of a 1–99 scale) or better to weed out the weaker stocks. Many of the best rate 90 to 99.

N—NEW PRODUCTS, NEW MANAGEMENT, NEW PRICE HIGHS

New products and new services are tied to a stock's performance. Buy at new price highs coming out of sound chart base patterns. You want to buy when the price looks too high to the many and sell after it goes substantially higher and finally looks attractive to everyone else. You also would like to see something new, whether it is in management and/or new products or services that are introduced in order to spur demand for those companies' products. Many companies had IPO's in more recent years.

S—SUPPLY AND DEMAND

You want to seek out how many shares outstanding a company has and also look for large increases in volume as the stock makes new highs in price. This action implies a strong demand for the stock. Smaller capitalization stocks are easier to move up in price, and also down, which is why you need a strict loss-cutting rule. Also look for excessive stock splits, as most stocks will top out around their second or third split. A company's buying back its stock is also a plus, as it shows management has confidence in the stock. Low debt-to-equity ratios are sometimes desired, and strong volume on up days and lower volume on down days are preferred. The best performers had less than 25 million shares of capitalization. So you don't have to restrict yourself to large cap stocks. Many times the best gains come from the smaller issues, although many midcap stocks are also fine.

L—LEADER OR LAGGARD

Buy the strongest leaders of the best groups. Some of O'Neil's biggest winners (in long positions) were:

Syntex	1963
Pic-N-Save	1976–1983
Price Company	1982–1985

Franklin Resources	1985–1986
Genetech	1986–1987
Amgen	1990–1991
AOL	1998–1999
Charles Schwab	1998–1999
Sun Microsystems	1998–1999
Qualcomm	1999

A leading stock is the best in its group with the best earnings, ROE, and price action. The RS (relative strength) rating is a way to tell if the stock is a leader. It measures price performance against the general market for the past 52 weeks. The average was 87 (on a 1–99 scale) for the best stocks before they made their huge price advances. Growth stocks tend to correct 1½ to 2½ times the market. The best stocks tend to drop the least and are usually the leaders of the new bull market. You need to confine your buys to the top two or three stocks in the top industry groups. This forces you to buy the very best quality.

O'Neil also has proved that certain industry groups and the strength of the industry is a key trait of the very best stocks, as the other great traders also discovered. You want to be sure you're invested in the top 20 percent of the groups that are currently leading the market. Look for new price highs within the strongest groups. Also, look to see if the market is currently favoring big cap stocks or small cap stocks.

Studies show that 37 percent of a stock's price movement is directly related to its industry group and another 12 percent is related to the stock's sector. Therefore, nearly 50 percent of a stock's price movement can be attributed to the group that it is a part of. The sector is the broader category, and the industry group is more specific.

Also avoid buying stocks that don't have at least one more stock in the group showing strong performance. This is similar to Livermore's observation of how the best-performing leaders usually have peers in the same group also performing well. A true leading group will consist of several other stocks showing promising strength.

Use volume to measure demand, as that is your best indicator in the market of what the demand for stocks is. O'Neil has shown that institutional support drives 75 percent of the market activity. *IBD* shows volume percentage changes for all stocks. It shows the average of each stock's last 50 days of volume trading and daily volume percentage change, so you can quickly see where the current high-volume action is taking place.

An example of how groups react within the market was when the Gold group rose to the top of the market as a leading industry group in February 1973, right before the beginning of the bear market of 1973 and 1974. This served as a clue as to what was coming by observing market group action, as gold is historically viewed as a defensive industry. The stock market is like a giant mirror that reflects the basic conditions, political management and mismanagement, and the psychology of the country. It's crucial to understand this and know how groups and leaders act.

I—INSTITUTIONAL SPONSORSHIP

Make absolutely sure that at least one or two leading (best performing) institutions hold a stake in the stock you are considering and the stock shows an increasing number of institutions taking positions in recent quarters. Because institutions account for 75 percent of all relevant market activity, following their activity is crucial.

M—MARKET DIRECTION

This, even though it is listed last, is the most important element in the CAN SLIM method. It's the most important because you could be correct on all the others and miss this one when the market is not acting correctly, and you would have a hard time making gains. It is important to know which stage of the market you are in. Because 75 percent of all stocks tend to follow the lead of the market, it is crucial to always know the current environment. You need not be able to predict where it's going, but understanding exactly what it is doing currently is what counts.

As you can see, O'Neil places a great deal of emphasis on research. This is important. The market is not supposed to be easy. His proven methods have been devised from intense study of how the market actually operates, and he has created many unique resources for individual investors so they can assess quickly which stocks stand stronger than others as far as fundamentals and technicals are concerned. This is why it is crucial to study and read *IBD* on a daily basis.

There are other important stock traits that O'Neil has discovered that have been contributors to a stock's great price performance over many decades. Among them is relative strength (RS).

Measured against both the general market and against other stocks, *IBD*'s RS rating is the price of the stock calculated one year ago and then taking the current price and calculating the change and comparing that stock's RS to all others. This shows how strong, or weak, a stock is performing in price in relation to others and the market. The average RS of the best, since 1953, was 87 before they made their huge price advances. The rating is also based on a 1–99 scale, as are most of the other *IBD* proprietary ratings. O'Neil recommends a rating of at least 80 or higher. You need to understand and look for these stocks that gain in ground during down markets and constantly perform well against other stocks and the market.

Another trait is the accumulation/distribution rating, showing if a stock is being accumulated (bought) or being distributed (sold) by big institutional investors. *IBD* tracks the last 13 weeks of this activity in each stock. A sponsorship rating determines if funds and large investors have been buying or selling stock. Again, it is important to follow the lead of institutions that are taking positions in the leading growth stocks.

O'Neil's study of charts discovered certain price consolidation areas or specific base patterns that occurred over time. These patterns formed just before the stocks took off to reap large gains, and they have occurred over many different markets and many different time periods. Patterns are formed due to corrections in the overall market, and the charts of stocks graphically illustrate supply and demand for a stock. You must be able to understand chart reading in order to properly determine correct buy and sell points and properly determine when trends are changing. O'Neil keeps the vital aspects of charts simple, using basic price and volume as the key drivers. Like the others before him, the volume and price action of the stock are the best determinants of supply and demand. With all the other technical traits available, one need not get confused, but stick to the basics of price and volume.

O'Neil looks for patterns in stock charts that have repeated themselves over many time periods, and as Livermore also stated many years ago, patterns in stock action will repeat themselves over and over again. The most common pattern O'Neil discovered was what is called the Cup-with-Handle (see Figure 5-1). This pattern resembles the silhouette of a coffee cup from the side. It shows a sloping downward left side, a bottom, a rising right side, a handle, and then a pivot point that acts as the ideal time to purchase the stock as it breaks through that point at the handles' peak on an increase in volume.

The best stocks showed at least a 30-percent price uptrend before they began their Cup-with-Handle formations. The minimum time for this pattern to form was between 7 or 8 weeks, though some stocks take as long as 15 months. Most will decline between 20 percent to 30 percent from the absolute peak (point 1 in Figure 5-1) to the low of the cup (point 2). The handles (points 3 and 4) are usually short and last between 1 to 7 or 8 weeks and need to slant downward on decreasing and lower-than-average volume. This weeds out the remaining weak holders of the stock. The handle pullback should fall no more than 10 percent to 15 percent during bull markets.

The pivot point (point 5) resembles the point of least resistance. It is currently .10 of a point above the peak of the handle area. It is the new high of the handle but is typically below the actual old high of the stock. This pivot point becomes the point for the least amount of risk. After all the remaining skeptical stockholders are washed out, the stock is able to make new highs in price without overhead resistance. Volume should accelerate considerably (50 percent or greater than its average) when the stock breaks through this point. This confirms the strong demand for the stock and proves bigger investors have taken an interest in the stock.

Figure 5-1 is the chart of U.S. Surgical. Once it broke through its pivot point in April 1990 at $60 a share, it appreciated an impressive 767 percent over the next 22 months. The fundamentals of the company were also top-notch, and other leading medical stocks and medical groups were showing very strong leadership at the time.

Buying at new highs seems uncomfortable, but it's actually buying into emerging strength and is key to great potential gains. Again, we see

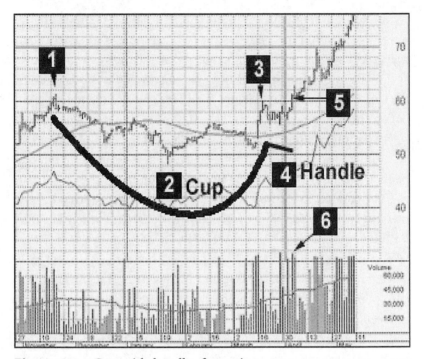

Figure 5-1   Cup-with-handle formation. Source: *www.investors.com* (*IBD* Learning Center)

a strategy of buying stocks near their highest prices, as opposed to buying at their lowest prices and looking for bargains. Even today, as the greats proved going back more than 100 years, this is the way to correctly time your buys for large gains, but is looked at as not being the correct way to purchase stocks by the majority of less knowledgeable investors.

O'Neil also proved this when he started creating his rules after analyzing the more than 100 stocks he studied with the Dreyfus Fund purchases of the late 1950s. All of them were purchased as each one established a new high in price after coming out of a base-forming pattern. The key is to concentrate on the leaders making new highs. Use the motto "buy high and sell a lot higher." Cheap stocks are cheap for a reason, and most will never make it back to their former high prices.

The next common chart pattern is the Double-Bottom base (see Figure 5-2). This looks like the letter "W." It's characterized by a price decline (points 1 and 2), then an initial upward trend (points 2 and 3), and then one more decline (points 3 and 4) before the stock returns to

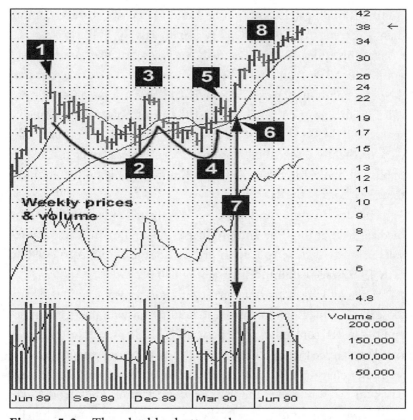

Figure 5-2 The double bottom base. Source:*www.investors.com* (*IBD* Learning Center).

its previous high (points 4 and 5). The right side of the W should drop slightly lower than the left side, as that shakes out the last remaining weak holders. The pivot point on a double bottom pattern is located on the top right side of the "W," where the stock is coming up after the second leg down (points 6 and 7). This point should be when the price surpasses the highest point in the handle by at least .10, or the peak price in the middle of the "W" when a handle has not occurred.

The stock illustrated in Figure 5-2 was American Power Conversion. After breaking though its pivot point and crossing $22 a share, it zoomed to an 800-percent increase over the next 22 months. It also sported first-class fundamentals before the stock broke out.

The next pattern is the Flat Base (Figure 5-3). This usually occurs as a second stage formation after a Cup-with-Handle base as the stock continues trading sideways (points 1 and 2) and not correcting more than 8 percent to 12 percent. They usually last for at least five or six weeks. This quiet action is actually very constructive. A new pivot point (point 3) is then established as you wait for the stock to rise past the pivot point on increased volume. Make sure not to chase the stock if it has already risen 5 percent past the pivot point, as you may be shaken out due to your loss-cutting rule if the stock temporarily falls back or slightly under the pivot point. Again, please refer to O'Neil's published books for greater detail and more graphic presentations of these key stock patterns.

The stock featured in Figure 5-3 is Amgen. It was a leader in the medical field at the time and produced outstanding fundamental results prior to its huge run-up in price. The stock, from April 1990 to early 1992, staged an impressive gain of 640 percent.

When looking at chart patterns, you should always avoid wide and loose bases as they are more prone to failure. Stay with the tighter bases and the better-controlled price patterns. This helps to minimize your risk. You can see these patterns fairly clearly the more you get better at analyzing charts and certain chart patterns. Also, avoid fourth-stage bases on the way up, as they are prone to failure. They tend to fail nearly 80 percent of the time. By the time a stock has formed a fourth-stage base, almost everyone has heard of the stock, and it will most likely lack future buying power.

A sound base in a stock has the following characteristics:

- Has more weeks up in price on greater than average volume than down weeks on greater volume
- Has shown some tight weeks showing little or no price change
- Has shown huge weekly spikes in volume on price increases once or twice within the last year or 12 months

O'Neil has shown that 40 percent of all stocks that break through their pivot points will fall back to the pivot point in their base. Some normal pullbacks after the pivot might include two or three down days in increased volume to the pivot point. Be patient and wait to see what happens, as this is a normal reaction. Also, if a stock trades under its

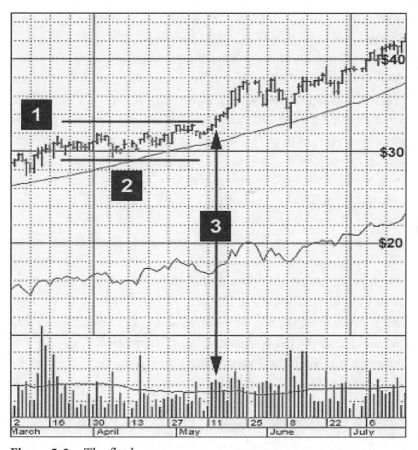

Figure 5-3   The flat base. Source: *www.investors.com* (*IBD* Learning Center).

50-day moving average line for only one or two days, this is also considered normal in many cases.

It's important to understand how these stocks behave as you analyze their price and volume action. Charts represent human nature and investor psychology and past actions. This does not change in the marketplace, and it will repeat itself over and over again in future markets, as history continuously repeats itself in the stock market. That is why it is important to understand that with proper study, analysis, and research in how to correctly interpret stock chart patterns, you can significantly increase your results.

Downtrends and bear markets are actually constructive for the market, as they create new bases for the next round of new leaders to emerge. So never give up when the market isn't acting right, and use bear markets to do more research and analysis.

As with the others, one of O'Neil's crucial trading rules is to follow the general trend of the market. In following the general market, it is important to understand what it is currently doing and look for tops when it has been rising for some time. Because most stocks follow the general market, four or five distribution days (heavy selling) in the market averages over a two- to four-week period could signal a top in the general market. This is when you stop buying stocks and begin looking to sell stocks. Market tops always give signals to the alert traders and astute investors.

History has shown that markets have given plenty of sell signals and topping signs in advance of their major collapses. It's the hope of investors that usually will prevent them from spotting these signals or cause them to ignore them, leading to increased losses. The best time to sell stocks is on the way up in price, when they are still advancing and looking strong to everyone else. Another great sell signal is to notice when you are tickled to death and happy as can be.

After declining for some time, markets always recover and come back. This was Baruch's favorite time to take action in the market. The astute trader needs to look for market bottoms and the confirmations off the bottom. Bottoms will usually occur after the corrections of bear markets with an increase in the major averages from the prior day. After the initial up day, four to seven days into the rally you need to look for a follow-through confirmation, as mentioned earlier. These initial rallies do have a 20-percent failure rate. The best big stock winners usually emerge during the first 10 to 15 weeks of a new bull market. There is simply no substitute for success, and one of the leading factors in stock trading is understanding day to day what the market is currently doing.

The pyramiding strategy that others used is also a key trading rule of O'Neil. He adds more to his initial purchase after the stock acts correctly from his first purchase. If the stock moves up 2½ percent to 3 percent from his buy point, he will buy additional shares and average up. He advises this pyramid approach, and it has attributed to large gains for him throughout his career. For example, if you want to invest $20,000 in one issue, you should buy half or $10,000 on the initial purchase. If the stock moves up 2½ percent to 3 percent, then you buy the next round of $6500, and if it continues to move up, then you purchase the last $3500. This pyramiding up and allocation of the initial intended amount to invest is a prudent leverage strategy that many of the others also proved for realizing increased returns.

O'Neil believes it's best to work with dollar amounts as opposed to the number of shares. If you have a successful position and are showing a substantial profit, then you can add more shares as the stock builds another base or bounces off its 50-day moving average, assuming it has not violated any of the other sell rules. It's also important to never let a gain turn into a loss. His profitable experience in Pic-N-Save was achieved as he continued to buy on the way up. He bought that stock 285 different times over 7½ years. The early purchases in that stock realized him a twentyfold gain.

O'Neil's buying rules could be summed up as follows:

- Concentrate on listed stocks trading at least $20 per share or Nasdaq leaders $15 and higher that have institutional support
- EPS should have increases in each of the past three years, and the current quarterly earnings must be up at least 20 percent
- Stock should be about to make a new high in price emerging from a sound basing pattern and be accompanied by at least a 50-percent increase in their volume for the day

He doesn't buy stocks trading under $15 per share, as he believes that cheap stocks are cheap for a reason. The study he conducted going back to 1953 discovered that the average price, before the greatest stocks started their major price moves, was $28 per share. Typical investors love low-priced stocks. O'Neil does not.

He also usually doesn't recommend purchasing IPO's (initial public offerings) because they have not established proper bases and trading patterns yet. The best time to buy fundamentally strong new issues is when they are coming out of their first established base on a break-out, usually two or three months after the IPO. The majority of the best performers, he discovered through his research, are stocks that came public within the prior eight years.

To sum up all of the research he has conducted, he offers three keys to success:

- Have a set of buying rules that limit your purchases to only the best and fundamentally strong companies. Use charts to determine the correct time to buy these potential leaders.

- Have a set of selling rules. Cut all losses short at 7 percent to 8 percent below your cost. Learn how to take your worthwhile profits according to your sell rules.

- Learn how to read the general market and be able to decipher what stage the market is currently in and try not to predict what it will do. Study it every day.

And his three basic overall rules are:

- Specific strategies for stock selection
- Rigorous risk control
- Discipline not to deviate from the two above

As for short selling, he believes it is hard to succeed at and should only be performed by the most experienced traders. If you do try shorting, you should only confine your short transactions to bear markets and limit your losses and don't short small capitalization stocks or stocks you think are too high in price. The two best chart patterns to use for shorting are the head and shoulder top and third- or fourth-stage basing patterns.

There will always be less-successful investors, some academics, competitors, or a few "know-it-all" cynics who will confidently claim that charts don't work. They say you can't time the market; CAN SLIM won't work; cutting losses is bad advice; averaging down is OK...just buy low, diversify widely, be a buy-and-hold investor; dividends, book value, and low PE's are what's important.

O'Neil's 40 years of results have proven conventional wisdom to be exceedingly faulty and, at times, extremely risky. The CAN SLIM method has also produced a number of millionaires. If you attend one of his Advanced Investment Workshops, you'll usually meet a number of long-term advocates who will be up 50 to over 100 percent for the year in any decent market period.

The American Association of Individual Investors has performed an independent, real-time, study monthly since 1998 of more than 50 of the best-known methods of investing. It stated, "The long-term leader in the growth category continues to be the O'Neil CAN SLIM approach, generating a 503-percent gain over the past 5 ½ years without a single down year." The results of their objective, validating study appeared in their *AAII Journal* of August 2003.

William O'Neil has dedicated his career to the meticulous study of the stock market. His hard work has definitely paid off, as his success has earned him a highly respectable reputation in the securities business and has afforded him wealth. Many individual investors, myself included, have many thanks to give to O'Neil for all the fact-based information he has provided to independent investors and stock traders. One could only imagine how much better the results of Livermore, Baruch, Loeb, and Darvas would have been had they had access to O'Neil's research, proprietary stock database, and tools such as *Investor's Business Daily* and the companion Web site *www.investors.com.*

Figures 5-4 through 5-7 show five-year stock performance graphs of O'Neil's biggest winners in the late 1990s. The charts illustrate at a glance how clearly one can see price and volume action in these stocks. They are not intended to show O'Neil's exact buy and sell points of these stocks. Rather, you can that see that in 1998 and 1999, these stocks were making large gains on increased volume activity. Also, the general market was in a very strong uptrend, and these stocks were the leaders at that time. The charts clearly illustrate how leaders can propel upward when the market environment is in a strong uptrend. The charts show all the way out through the first quarter of 2003. They demonstrate that with no loss-cutting strategy in place, or profit-taking rules, the large gains made in the

America Online Chart 1998–2003

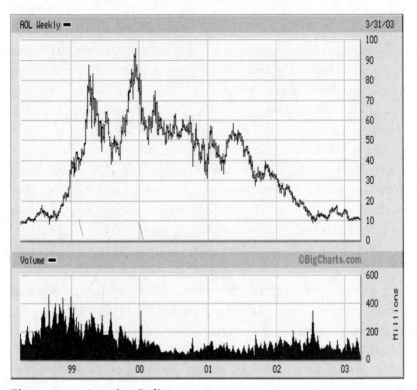

Figure 5-4   America Online. Source: *www.bigcharts.com.*

late 1990s would have been completely wiped out if the investor had held on for the long term as opposed to taking the market cues of when to exit a profitable stock. O'Neil was out of these stocks near the top and kept his substantial gains, while buy and holders stood by in disbelief as their once mighty paper gains faded away and turned into substantial losses.

Qualcomm Chart 1998–2003

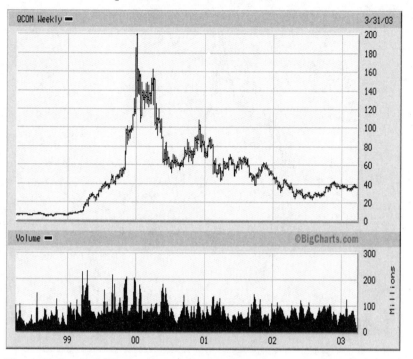

Figure 5-5   Qualcomm. Source: *www.bigcharts.com.*

Sun Microsystems Chart 1998–2003

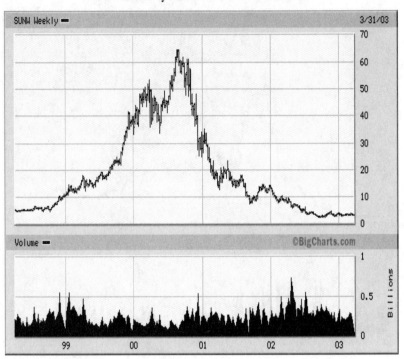

Figure 5-6   Sun Microsystems. Source: *www.bigcharts.com.*

Charles Schwab Chart 1998–2003

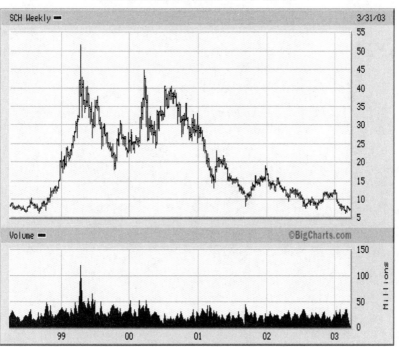

Figure 5-7 Charles Schwab & Co. Source: *www.bigcharts.com.*

6

Strategies of the Greatest Traders

After reviewing the profiles and strategies of these five successful stock traders that cover every year of the stock market from the early 1890s to the present, it is interesting to see how each of the traders adopted similar strategies and disciplines. As some of the chapters outlined, there were references made to the traders before them. For example, William J. O'Neil studied Gerald M. Loeb and Jesse Livermore extensively. He has mentioned them in past interviews, and he references many of their published works when he recommends books and reading material on the stock market and trading.

Darvas mentioned in the *Time* magazine interview that he would reread Loeb's classic *The Battle for Investment Survival* every two weeks just to stay disciplined to the rules. To him this resource was a valuable guide in helping him keep his focus. Each trader battled different market environments, though some overlapped certain years. The exception was Livermore and Baruch, both of whom were active at the same periods during their trading careers.

We read about how they all made mistakes early in their experiences and lost money, proving that they were human as well. We also saw that it does not take a great amount of capital to get started and to grow that capital into substantial wealth over time. Livermore started with only a few dollars (and that was in 1892), and O'Neil had only $500 when he placed his first trade.

The early years of their careers resulted in losses that drove each of these five traders to understand why, and to analyze the actions of the stocks that caused these losses. They proved that with the proper attitude and determination, learning from mistakes, and establishing rules that work, it is possible to attain the monetary rewards that many dream about as they enter the world of stock trading. One thing these great traders have proved is that it is not easy, and the belief that many have of making quick riches without much effort is a false one.

We will now examine the many common trading strategies each employed as they struggled through their early years, searching for ways to succeed in the market. During the many years these traders covered, common traits, disciplines, and trading rules applied to all of them.

Common Skills

The number-one skill required that was common to all these traders was a strong work ethic. We saw from each that the amount of effort, dedication, and work put forth in the effort to succeed was a crucial factor to the success of each. This should come as no surprise, as many mentioned that to become successful, and especially to attain the highest levels of success, it takes hard work to get to the top. It is no different than in any other profession. What is worth the rewards requires the efforts to gain the rewards.

All, except for Darvas, concluded that due to the effort that was required, it took one's full-time attention to the task. As mentioned, Darvas was the only one not involved in the securities or trading business on a full-time basis. But determination to succeed took most of his time outside his other profession. Actually, he mentioned that he spent eight hours a day studying the market. This for most would qualify as full time.

All learned that due to the hard work required to profit in the stock market, the rewards were not going to come overnight. Rather, the time element proved that, like most other rewarding endeavors, overnight success does not happen very often in the stock market. If and when it does occur, it usually doesn't last long without the proper attention, effort, and sound trading rules being implemented.

Observation and study were requirements. These were vital compliments to the hard work that was required. Each would study the market and look to understand the way the market reacts and how they could benefit from the opportunities in the actions of the market.

Each learned that experience was key. They learned from their mistakes just as they learned to pay attention to the varied lessons they learned along the way. The experience one gains as one heads down the path of any venture must be remembered so that when similar situations arise in the future, those experiences and memories can be recalled to avoid repeated mistakes. This is especially true in the market, as it has been shown that patterns repeat themselves in stocks and market behavior year after year and cycle after cycle.

All the traders featured here struggled with the enemy that every stock market participant experiences, which is uncontrolled emotions. The skill required is to be able to keep the emotions under control. In order to do this, all these traders created sound trading rules that worked well for them. By following strict rules, they were able to control the emotional part of trading that can overcome and cause rather normal, intelligent people to act in ways that they otherwise would not act if they did not have their hard-earned money on the line. Throughout this book, emotional control is discussed as a skill, a discipline, and a result of specific trading rules being implemented. The emotional balance, while active in the market, is simply a trait that the very best were able to control. In order to do this, you have to have real money on the line, and you need to experience sometimes gut-wrenching losses in order to understand how unrestrained emotions can become a stock trader's worst enemy.

Loeb and Darvas discussed certain personalities or characteristics that could be attributed to certain stocks. Loeb probably best described it as stocks having stages similar to those humans go through. Infancy, growth, maturity, and decline describe both stocks and humans. The best gains are made in the growth phase. O'Neil discovered that stocks followed certain patterns over time, that these patterns repeat themselves, and the best stocks have similar patterns and bases. Being able to identify certain patterns and at what stage a stock was in contributed to each of their successes.

Having the drive to attain high goals and success was a trait common to these great traders. Loeb and Darvas especially would comment that it was vital to them to have very aggressive goals and aim for the highest returns possible. Livermore, Baruch, and O'Neil obviously had the drive and perseverance to push themselves to the limits in obtaining their goals as well.

Sound judgment and thought, common sense, and humility are key skills one must employ in participating successfully in the ever-challenging environment of the market. Intelligence definitely helps and is required, but one does not need the highest levels of intelligence to succeed in the market. In fact, higher intelligence can sometimes lead to ego and overconfidence problems, which can be devastating and costly in the stock market.

Finally, the skill of being able to react quickly and the ability to change was key to all of their successes. Though Livermore was quoted as saying that the markets never really change due to human nature, the markets do change in the sense that they adapt to new companies, new improvements in business, economics, and world events. His statement related to how people react to events, which does not change much due to certain human traits. Due to market cycle changes, one must be able to react to these changes. As opposed to the buy-and-holders, who purchase a stock and hold it forever, many recently have discovered that the inability to change and react with the market can be extremely costly. Enron, WorldCom, and many more over the years and decades were once regarded as blue chip companies. Those who purchased and ignored the market environment and the action in the stocks that declined significantly and then became unlisted and names for the history books will certainly not make the list of distinguished names in this book.

The skills listed above were discovered by all these traders in their quest for success. Most are basic and seem logical; the difficulty is admitting they need to be employed and refined with hard work, trial and error, and many years of effort.

Shared Disciplines

All of these traders discovered that being disciplined in their behaviors and their approach to the market contributed to the control over their emotions, which led to rational actions utilizing sound and proven trading strategies. This discipline is learned over time, as they all experienced setbacks in the early days. Discipline became part of the learning process and was used to force them into adhering to the rules of each of their methods.

All shared the same thoughts on how tips and so-called inside information was a hazardous way to trade in stocks. Everybody, it seems, has an opinion about some stock and knows of some hot tip. It's the source of the information that should always be questioned. Many of these traders all learned the hard way about taking advice from others. Livermore lost plenty listening to the Cotton King, Percy Thomas. Baruch lost all of his original capital, and a significant amount of his father's as well, by listening to a tip from an outsider. By seeking opinions from others, Darvas consistently lost money after his first profitable success from the Brilund stock.

These experiences and more led all to believe that probably the most important discipline is to do your own research and do not listen to others and their opinions. Each one learned from reading on their own and then being able to make their decisions and reach their own conclusions from studying the market, history, charts, etc., and then constantly learning from real-life experiences. They all believed that no one can master the market, but traders could succeed financially if they worked hard, kept learning as they went along, and did their own research.

Even Gerald Loeb, in 1965, updated his classic *The Battle for Investment Survival*, originally published in 1935, with new ideas he had learned over the next 30 years. William J. O'Neil believed so strongly in the discipline to do one's own research that he founded *Investor's Business Daily*, so the independent individual investor can have a resource to conduct unbiased, fact-based research. Even today, some 70 years after the creation of the Securities and Exchange Commission, we still have advice and information coming from some of the oldest and supposedly most distinguished investment houses that is inaccurate, misleading, and found to be outright worthy of fines, penalties, and banishment of analyst personnel from the industry. Investors simply must be able to conduct their own unbiased research, and these great traders have proven that it can be done very successfully.

Another common discipline among all five traders was that they all did a hard analysis of each of their trades. For a trader, this is one of the hardest disciplines to adhere to, but when one does begin and sticks to it, it becomes an important learning tool. When these traders lost money, they didn't blame the market or their stocks. They looked at their own actions and decided to analyze what they did that caused their losses.

This statement is important. You must have the ability to take responsibility for all of your own trades, and not look at the market as the reason for your loss. It simply is not worth it to get angry with the market.

Instead, these traders learned that the key to reducing losses and getting on the road to profits is to constantly analyze the trades one makes, and then learn from the mistakes. They understood their successes so they could eliminate the loss-causing actions and capitalize on the transactions that led to the profitable gains. All would write down when they made their trades, and they would go back later and review them, especially the losing trades. It's not easy to admit and then keep looking at your mistakes as a reminder, but it helps in the constant learning process, and these greats all proved that fact.

In doing their own research, all of them made sure they were silent about their trades. Livermore and Darvas even mention using multiple brokers to conduct their trades, as they did not want anyone to be able to track their actions. Loeb was so silent about his trades that he didn't even mention his specific trades in his publications. O'Neil makes sure not to offer recommendations in the daily editions of *IBD* or publicize his current positions.

It's one thing to have some winners in the stock market that provide some real profits; it's another challenge to keep them. Setting up a reserve account was another common discipline with all the great traders. Baruch, Loeb, and Darvas all took some of their profits off the table and put them away for reserve. O'Neil funneled his early profits into other strategic investments, such as a seat on the New York Stock Exchange, his own investment research firm, and then the founding of *Investor's Business Daily.* Livermore struggled with this discipline more than the others, but was rumored to have finally established a fund later in his trading career to avoid the times before where he gave back the bulk of his gains.

The reserve account is the ammunition and inventory for the stock trader. In order to be able to react quickly when the market changes, or when new and better stock opportunities arise, the cash from a reserve account allows the prudent trader to take advantage of those market opportunities. The reserve account also adheres to another discipline of these traders, the ability to be able to stay away from the market when it is wise to do so.

All thought that being in the market all the time was not a prudent trading strategy. The market simply does not always offer the most opportune environment. Loeb and Darvas didn't believe in being in the market during downtrends or bear markets, and neither does O'Neil. Livermore didn't think sideways markets gave any opportunities for profit, as he looked for activity either on the upside or the downside. Being out of the market allows one to step away and refocus and then enter again when better opportunities present themselves. This quiet time out of the market also gave these traders time to do additional analysis of the market and price trends.

The discipline of constant analysis while out of the market is like a top athlete training during the off season. You stay on top of your game and make sure you are prepared when it's time to trade again.

A key discipline of all these great traders that goes against almost all broker and investment advice that most hear regards the topic of diversification. Many investors are told to diversify their investments in order to reduce risk. Every single one of these five traders could not disagree more. In fact, they all believed that the most profits could be made in diversifying as little as possible, and they proved it by making millions.

They all discovered through their many years of mistakes and experience that by trading and holding only a handful of quality U.S.-based stocks that trade on the major exchanges, if purchased correctly, during the right market environments, and then sold correctly, one could make a fortune. This discipline to stay focused on just a few of the leading stocks that were experiencing the highest demand at the time, and not diversifying into all kinds of different investments that they were not experts at, led them all to incredible wealth. Gerald Loeb said it best, "The greatest safety lies in putting all your eggs in one basket and watching that basket."

Relating to diversification in the sense of knowing what you are investing in, these traders knew the importance of having knowledge of what they were trading in. Baruch was a firm believer in doing as much research about a company as possible. He attributed one of the main reasons for his losses to his lack of knowledge about the companies he invested in. O'Neil puts a great deal of emphasis on the fundamentals of a company, as *IBD* supplies the investor with many fundamental statistics so one can more quickly conduct qualified research. Disciplining yourself to know who the quality leaders are and understanding the market environment are key ingredients to successful stock trading.

Another key discipline that these traders employed that goes against some of the more popular opinions concerning investments is the issue of tax considerations. The traders who came along later, such as Loeb, Darvas, and O'Neil, all regarded tax considerations as secondary to first making as large a profit as possible, and then thinking about how tax considerations would affect the trade. Many today might hold a winning stock, and after it declines and shows classic sell signals, they hold on and wait for a favorable tax consideration period. In the meantime their profits might be totally wiped out due to the waiting period. The very best traders concentrate on profits first and look at tax considerations second.

It is clear that many of the disciplines that were vital to the success of these traders went against the grain of conventional and popular thinking when it came to stocks. Like some other things in life, sometimes it's best to take the road less traveled. If these traders have proven for over 100 years that these similar disciplines have worked, maybe it's time more traders started to adopt them if their aim is to make large profits in the market.

Common Trading Rules

A major key to profitable stock trading over many years requires sound trading rules that have been refined through experience and fit the individual's strengths. All five of these great traders created rules that kept them out of bad markets and gave them the signals to take advantage of profitable opportunities when the market presented them. It is a must requirement to adhere to strict trading rules in order to manage risk in the ever-challenging stock market. Their rules were created and adjusted as they kept learning, analyzing, and trying new ways until the results began to show positive returns. Again, we will see that as each went through the same trials, even though there were different periods of time involved, many discovered that similar rules resulted in similar outcomes. This again proves that the market repeats itself and that historical patterns have occurred again and again and will occur in the future as well.

The number-one trading rule for all was the rule of limiting their losses when they had them. It was repeated over and over again in each chapter, and it's repeated numerous times in each of their publications. There is simply no better risk control trading rule than to accept a small loss when you have one and move on to the next stock if an opportunity presents itself. The ability to cut your losses quickly is what separates the best traders from everybody else.

Even the greatest traders featured in this book, the very best and most successful over time, experienced loss ratios of near 50 percent. Because no one will be correct every time, it's the ability to enforce this rule that keeps the profits in the expert traders' accounts and leaves the amateurs in disbelief, as they watch their stock keep going down in price and do nothing about it. They refuse to sell because they consider themselves long-term investors, or they have a tip from an expert and there is no way that their stock could decline in price, or because they work for the company, etc. This can create havoc on an individual portfolio.

Livermore and Baruch would limit their initial losses to 10 percent, due to the margin requirements at the time. This automatic rule would force them out, if they were on margin, so there was no holding on forever and wishing and hoping for a rebound from a larger loss. Early on they both violated this rule when not using margin, but then soon learned that the loss-cutting strategy was a crucial rule in keeping their earnings. Loeb and Darvas both mentioned that they cut their losses under 10 percent. Their strict adherence to this rule allowed them both to keep their profits. O'Neil constantly reminds traders in his books and in *Investor's Business Daily*, that the loss cutting rule is the number one trading rule. He advocates cutting losses quickly at 7 percent to 8 percent below your purchase price. He has mentioned that he actually averages less than that due to his experience, probably in the 3-percent to 5-percent range.

With experience, all these great traders cut their losses under their specified maximum limits. If you constantly study the market and see action that does not look right after you're in a position, there is no reason to wait around for an 8-percent to 10-percent loss. Take it quickly and move on to the next opportunity. Even through intense study and years of experience, you just will not avoid losses, as the odds and market environment do not allow for a perfect stock-picking record.

Even the best hitters in baseball only succeed 30 percent of the time. Baruch said it best, "No speculator can be right all the time. In fact, if a speculator is correct half of the time, he is hitting a good average. Even being right three or four times out of ten should yield a person a fortune if he has the sense to cut his losses quickly on the ventures where he has been wrong." Many recent investors and traders have learned this lesson the hard way since March 2000, when the market peaked, and they held on to watch all their gains evaporate and turn into devastating losses as they failed to cut their losses short.

Emotions have been mentioned many times as they can overcome a trader and lead to inappropriate actions that eventually lead to losses. All these traders recognized the danger of letting emotions take over, and that is the reason they all created their own rules. The rules are used as a replacement to the unpredictability of the emotional trader. Traders without rules will eventually succumb to emotional trading, which has proved to be a loser's game time and time again. The removal and control of emotions cannot be stated enough to get the point across of the dangers they represent and can cause.

Probably just as important as the loss-cutting rule was the understanding of how important it was to know what the general market was doing at the time they decided to enter and exit their trades. Ignoring general market behavior is a lesson one will learn the hard way and it's been proven again during the tough market environment starting in the spring of 2000 through 2002. Those trying to buy against the grain of a bear market soon learn how difficult it can be to try to go against the momentum of the market. All these traders discovered, through their analysis, how most stocks react to the direction of the general market.

Livermore would always stay out of market trends that were indecisive or sideways. He would always make sure the market led first, and then he would trade accordingly. Baruch discovered the best opportunities were when a market changed directions coming off a correction, and he would buy into the new emerging strength of an upturn. Loeb and Darvas learned to stay out of declining or bear markets. They would stay observant and gradually buy into leading stocks as the market began to change directions. O'Neil constantly emphasizes the importance of watching the general market. The "M" in his CAN SLIM strategy, he mentions, is the most important element to watch, and his studies show that approximately 75 percent of all stocks follow the direction of the general market. With those odds, it simply does not make sense to try to make gains on stock purchases when the general trend is not going in the same direction.

As we saw earlier, many of the trading rules that these traders implemented went against the popular opinions of what was and is thought to be the correct way to invest in the stock market. It's hard to argue with the success of their results, but many still refuse to accept that their methods and rules can result in profitable gains. Probably the most controversial rule that these traders enforced was that they would only buy stocks when they reached a new high in price.

Livermore, Loeb, Darvas, and O'Neil all discovered that the best gains came when certain stocks would move past certain pivotal points and into new high ground. How different does this rule seem when most think that the old saying of "buy low and sell high" is the correct way to trade in the market, when in fact, that strategy did not contribute to the millions of dollars in profits that these great traders were able to produce. Rather, their strategies were based on a "buy high and sell a lot higher" premise. They all thought that cheap stocks were cheap for a reason, and that they usually get cheaper.

In fact, Livermore would like to sell short stocks that were making new lows. He believed that if they had fallen that low, then they would most likely keep going lower. Livermore was also one of the first traders to buy stocks as they made new highs in price after crossing certain resistance levels. Loeb, Darvas, and O'Neil also discovered through their own analysis that that rule would apply in the markets they traded in as well.

Another rule common to these traders was the use of pyramiding. Again, this rule goes against a popular view years ago and still prevalent today of averaging down, which is buying more of stock as it keeps declining. Pyramiding, as mentioned throughout this book, is the process of buying more of a rising stock as it keeps increasing in price. This strategy allowed all of them to leverage their winning stocks, when their action would convince them when they were correct, and to compound their gains by purchasing more of a strong stock as it kept getting stronger.

Each would continue buying at certain points until they were fully invested in the amount they had planned for that issue. Dedicated attention and observation to what the market's action was doing at the current time led each to employ this profitable strategy. They all proved for over 100 years that if done correctly, pyramiding one's strong stocks is the main key to realizing large profits.

Another mistake most traders make (that these greats did not) is to always look for the old leaders when the market turns up again. The former leaders of the prior bull market are rarely the same leaders of the new bull market. This makes sense, as the economy and business conditions change and lead to new opportunities of expected large future profits.

Many investors make the mistake of looking for the same old names that might have provided them profits in an earlier market cycle. Sometimes this might happen, but more often than not, it's new innovative companies that lead the next leg of the market to new heights. This too has been experienced over many decades, as each has produced its share of names that were standout performers. Study and observation of the market and new emerging leaders give the observant and reactionary trader the early jump when the market eventually starts a new uptrend.

Volume in the market and stocks is sometimes discarded as unimportant by some. The great traders did not see it that way. They looked at increases in volume on strong up days in a stock or the market as the most illustrative picture of strong demand. Volume therefore is the convincing element that there is an interest in an issue and, that with other certain parameters, is a requirement for a stock to keep increasing in price. These increases in volume for a stock as it was coming through a resistance level and through a pivotal point was the clearest signal yet that strength was being directed to that stock. They would jump on board after noticing this tremendous interest in a stock.

Of the many selling rules each of these traders implemented in their own strategies, one they each agreed on and one that was a major contributor to their large gains, was to hold on to their winners and not sell them too quickly. Many of them learned this lesson, as their early trading tended not to produce large gains because they were simply selling leading stocks too quickly in order to realize a small gain.

All discovered that no one could buy at the lowest possible price and sell at the highest possible price. They would all sell into the strength of a stock, as that is when all the smart money is selling. Livermore, Baruch, and Loeb were all mostly out of the market when the Great Crash occurred in October 1929. As mentioned earlier, Livermore saw it coming and shorted the market and had his best payday. They left the market before a major correction occurred, selling their rising positions on the way up or selling their profitable positions when they began to top and started to decline. Instead of holding on and wishing and hoping, they followed the action and reacted accordingly.

Darvas would always be out of a profitable stock as it began to decline significantly due to his stop loss orders. O'Neil mentions how he was out of the 1987 market in August, as leading stocks and the market gave their topping signals. He therefore avoided the miserable day of October 19, 1987 when the Dow fell more than 20 percent in one day. In the spring and fall of 2000, *IBD* constantly reminded investors that the leading stocks and general market were showing classic distribution signals.

As for shorting the market, Livermore and Baruch made substantial profits from short positions, as did O'Neil in the early 1960s with Korvette and Certain-teed. Loeb and Darvas were not very active in shorting, as they mentioned the general uptrend of the market over time and the more dangerous risks involved in shorting stocks. O'Neil does not advocate shorting except for the most experienced traders. He also mentions the increased risk involved and has proved that there are many great opportunities if one waits for the next bull market.

Conclusion

Lessons from the Greatest Stock Traders of All Time

We have reviewed the profiles, strategies, trading rules, and similarities of the greatest stock traders of all time. These traders were chosen due to their success in the market that included many years and many decades of profits. The published works that detail their strategies were all well received, and many became bestsellers.

As with most publications that use *the greatest* in their title, no matter which topic or profession it might represent, there will be arguments for the ones included and for the ones not included that many think should have been. The profiles chosen were based on active stock traders that began their careers, or added to them, while trading for their own accounts. They were also chosen as they covered each era of the market going back to the 1890s.

It's always interesting to see how great performers can attain success dealing within a similar environment over many different economic, social, political, and innovative time periods. As mentioned in the Introduction, there have no doubt been many successful stock traders over the years, and there have been many different strategies and approaches to the market that have produced profitable results. Many individuals are private traders who wish to retain their privacy. Others have been very successful in managing money for others as professional mutual fund or hedge fund managers.

Probably the most notable and one of the most successful was Peter Lynch. Lynch achieved incredible success as manager of The Fidelity Magellan Fund from 1977 to 1990. His publications *One Up on Wall Street* and *Beating the Street* are very good books for stock traders to read and study. Of course, there is also Warren Buffett. He has achieved fame and incredible wealth from his long-term investments due to his buy and hold strategy and his management ownership positions in the many companies he has invested in over the years.

It is, however, hard to argue with the innovative strategies and success that active traders Jesse Livermore, Bernard Baruch, Gerald Loeb, Nicolas Darvas, and William O'Neil have had on the stock market. Each one, through determination to succeed, learned what it ultimately took to stay on the profitable side of the market. Their efforts are truly evidence that being detailed and hard working in their approach can pay mighty rewards.

They proved that the stock market is not an easy place to find riches, but with perseverance and hard efforts, it's possible to succeed profitably over the long term. We saw as we went along the time scale that more attention to detail was available in their published works. Darvas's book *How I Made $2,000,000 in the Stock Market* illustrates charts of his best trades, showing his purchase and sell points. O'Neil's publications, especially *How to Make Money in Stocks*, details his trading strategies and rules with many charts of past winners. *Investor's Business Daily* and his Web site, *www.investors.com* are great resources that daily educate on how the market actually works and illustrates many real examples to support his strategies.

The most amazing discovery one should gain from this book is that even though these great traders conducted their activities in many different time periods on Wall Street, they would ultimately discover many of the same basic skills, disciplines, and trading rules that were required to achieve their success.

The main reason I decided to write this book was because I, like most, have made almost every mistake in the book when it comes to stock trading. As I constantly studied more and refused to give up, the best books I read are listed in the Bibliography/Resource section at the back of this book. I kept coming back to sections of these books and decided that it would be convenient to have one resource covering all the basics from the very best traders. I also discovered the many similarities in their approach to the market.

It was difficult to argue with their success, and I believed that if they could achieve great results over that many years covering all those different market environments, then there had to be some credence to their efforts. What was discovered is that the market demands intense and serious attention to the details, only if you want to profit from it. Hard work through observation and study, extreme discipline, patience, and the ability to implement sound trading rules in order to gain emotional control is what all these great traders discovered and led to their success.

Bibliography/Resources

Jesse Livermore

Lefevre, Edwin. *Reminiscences of a Stock Operator.* John Wiley & Sons, Inc. 1994. Originally published in 1923 by George H. Doran and Company. Copyright © 1993, 1994 by Expert Trading, Ltd. Foreword © 1994 by John Wiley & Sons, Inc. This material is used by permission of John Wiley & Sons, Inc.

Sarnoff, Paul. *Jesse Livermore: Speculator-King.* Copyright © 1967 by Paul Sarnoff. All rights reserved. Reprinted by permission by Traders Press, Inc. 1985.

Wyckoff, Richard D. *Jesse Livermore's Methods of Trading in Stocks.* Windsor Books. 1984. Copyright © 1984 by Windsor Books. Select material used by permission of Windsor Books.

Bernard Baruch

Baruch, Bernard. *My Own Story.* Buccaneer Books, Inc. 1957. Reprinted by arrangement with Henry Holt and Company. Copyright © 1957 by Bernard M. Baruch.

Grant, James. *Bernard M. Baruch: The Adventures of a Wall Street Legend.* John Wiley & Sons, Inc. 1997. Copyright © 1997 by James Grant. This material is used by permission of John Wiley & Sons, Inc.

Gerald M. Loeb

Loeb, Gerald M. *The Battle for Investment Survival.* Excerpts reprinted with permission of Simon & Schuster Adult Publishing Group. Copyright © 1935, 1936, 1937, 1943, 1952, 1953, 1954, © 1955, 1956, 1957 by Gerald M. Loeb. Copyright © 1965, and renewed © 1993, by H. Harvey Scholten.

Loeb, Gerald M. *The Battle for Stock Market Profits.* Excerpts reprinted with permission of Simon & Schuster Adult Publishing Group. Copyright © 1971 by H. Harvey Scholten.

Nicolas Darvas

Darvas, Nicolas. *How I Made $2,000,000 in the Stock Market.* Lyle Stuart books published by Kensington Publishing Corp. 1986. Copyright © 1986 Lyle Stuart, Inc. Copyright © 1994, 1971, 1960 Nicolas Darvas. All rights reserved. Reprinted by permission of Citadel Press/Kensington Publishing Corp. *www.kensingtonbooks.com*

Darvas, Nicolas. *Wall Street: The Other Las Vegas.* Lyle Stuart books published by Kensington Publishing Corp. Copyright © 1964, Nicolas Darvas. All rights reserved. Reprinted by permission of Citadel Press/Kensington Publishing Corp. *www.kensingtonbooks.com*

"Pas de Dough" *TIME,* 5/25/59. Copyright © 1959, TIME Inc. Select material reprinted by permission.

William J. O'Neil

O'Neil, William J. *How to Make Money in Stocks.* McGraw-Hill. 2002. Copyright © 2002 by William J. O'Neil. Copyright ©1995, 1991, 1988 by McGraw-Hill, Inc. All rights reserved.

O'Neil, William J. *24 Essential Lessons for Investment Success.* McGraw-Hill. 2000. Copyright © 2000 by William J. O'Neil. All rights reserved.

O'Neil, William J. *The Successful Investor.* McGraw-Hill. 2004. Copyright © 2004 by William J. O'Neil. All rights reserved.

Charts

www.bigcharts.com

www.investors.com (*IBD* Learning Center)

Resources Recommended for Daily Market Education

Investor's Business Daily

www.investors.com

INDEX

About the Author

John Boik is a controller and the owner of Stock Traders Management, Inc., a private money management firm. An active trader and former stockbroker, Boik writes the popular and influential column *The Stock Market Weekly Report* for Traders Press.